No X-Cuses!

Bob & Fran,

May God bless you.

No X-Cuses!

ADDRESSING THE SPIRITUAL, PHYSICAL, AND MENTAL/
EMOTIONAL COMPONENTS OF OUR LIVES

Mark

—Isaiah 40:31

MARK BEECHAM

authorHOUSE®

AuthorHouse™
1663 Liberty Drive
Bloomington, IN 47403
www.authorhouse.com
Phone: 1-800-839-8640

Published by AuthorHouse   08/24/2012

ISBN: 978-1-4772-6228-3 (sc)
ISBN: 978-1-4772-6227-6 (hc)
ISBN: 978-1-4772-6229-0 (e)

Library of Congress Control Number: 2012915190

It is not the critic who counts, not the man who points out how the strong man stumbles, or where the doer of deeds could have done them better. The credit belongs to the man who is actually in the arena, whose face is marred by dust and sweat and blood; who strives valiantly; who errs, who comes short again and again, because there is no effort without error and shortcoming; but who does actually strive to do the deeds; who knows great enthusiasms, the great devotions; who spends himself in a worthy cause; who at the best knows in the end the triumph of high achievement, and who at the worst, if he fails, at least fails while daring greatly, so that his place shall never be with those cold and timid souls who neither know victory nor defeat.

Theodore Roosevelt (1858-1919)
26th President of the United States
The Man in the Arena
Paris, France
April 23, 1910

ACKNOWLEDGEMENTS

W. Somerset Maugham once wrote, "We do not write because we want to; we write because we have to." This statement stokes the fire within my heart. As much as I would love to put off the writing of this book, I cannot do it. There is within my bones a desire to share the wit, wisdom, successes, and failures I and others have experienced.

During the recent few years, a proverb has become my life's theme. Proverbs 18:21 states, "The tongue has the power of life and death, and those who love it will eat its fruit." As you read the daily selections found in this book, my prayer is that you would speak its truth. As you speak its truth, may your life find more power and vitality than ever before experienced.

No one has ever seen a dream become reality without the help of others. It would be totally inappropriate to produce this work without acknowledging some very important people in my life.

The book would be far less complete without giving acknowledgement to one who has motivated me by his words and his actions. I have known Les Brown for many years through books and recordings; however, during the past few years, I was able to spend some time with him at his speaker's workshops. I have found him to be one whose message and life are congruent. Thanks you Les for sharing your heart.

Chuck Chappell is the kind of friend that everyone looks for. He is kind, compassionate, and loyal. Our friendship started in the third grade (Over thirty five years ago)! Although in many ways we are total opposites, our friendship has stood the test of time. Many people will spend their whole lives looking for a faithful friend, but I found mine in the third grade. We have been through it all together.

During the writing of this book, my friend, Beau Griffith, lost her husband to a heart attack. Tim was way too young to die. He was only 42. Beau's support and motivation made this book possible.

I also lost another friend while I was working on this book. My friend, Don Austin, died of a brain tumor. Even in the middle of the battle, he always kept his convictions. I am grateful to Don for sharing his "bulldog mentality." His friendship, love, and support will always have a special place in my heart.

Dr. Dianne Sawyer empowered me to write. I never knew I had it in me. After reading my first book's manuscript, she encouraged me by saying, "You have a gift of written communication." Thanks, Dr. Sawyer. I am doing my best to use that gift.

This book is also written in tribute to a special man who passed away recently. Johnny Adams was a man who lived his convictions daily. If I ever become half the man he was, I will consider myself a major success. I am so thankful that my path crossed his at a young age. By watching him, I learned how to live and how to love people. Hopefully, part of his spirit will live on through me.

I know I have probably failed to mention someone. However, please know I have been blessed to have so many friends who have graciously added to my life. Thanks for spending time with me and sharing your life. Life is short. Live your dreams!!

Mark Beecham
March 15, 2012

PREFACE

Why a 42-day motivational guide? That was a question asked of me by an inquiring person. What is significant about 42 days? There is nothing mystical about a 42-day period. The 42-day period is something which has become meaningful within my own life.

One of the people who has made a lasting impact upon my life is Zig Ziglar. Many people know Zig because of his high-spirited motivational seminars. He has literally given people the tools to make lasting change in their lives. I am one of them.

During one of Zig's seminars, he made a statement that stuck in the recesses of my mind. He said, "It takes 21 days to make a habit." I pondered that thought over and over again. In just three weeks a person can create and enforce powerful habits to either change or destroy their lives.

I began to think. If 21 days can make a habit, then what would 42 days do? By solidifying positive habits for 42 days, one can totally change the direction of life. In just six weeks, a person can go from hap-hazzardly to whole-heartedly living life. If a person can create a habit in just three weeks, then I contend in just three more weeks a person can create a mental blueprint so in-depth that everything will be as natural as sleeping and eating. By solidifying positive habits, one can totally change the direction of his or her life, thus causing a complete role reversal in just six weeks.

So, here it is. As you begin the journey of this book, I invite you to really think about the habits that rule your life. Do you read enough? Do you exercise enough? Do you pray enough? What do you want to become an integral part of your life? Ponder these questions for they will become the foundation for the habits which you will need to develop.

You may not like to read. You may not like to write; however, this is a new day. The sunrise on your new life is dawning and from this day forward you will like to read and write. I am glad you have that attitude. Say it aloud, "I love to read and write!" For the next 42 days, you will need to read and write. A discipline that is practiced consistently by all successful people is reading and writing. Congratulations, you have just developed that trait. See, you are already on your way to a changed life!

It is my hope and prayer that after these 42 days you will be a new person. Your life has the potential, in the next 42 days, to become so focused, that you will never settle for anything except the best. You were created for success so do not accept anything less than the best. I offer to you the <u>No X-Cuses!</u> lifestyle. Will you take it? Will you live it? That answer lies within you.

Ernest Pearson, a great man and a good friend, constantly says, "We have to move from good to great!" You may be living a good life, but are you living a great life? Embrace the best for yourself; you deserve it, after all, you have been created in the image of the Most High God!!

ACCOUNTABILITY

This book is intended to change your life! In order for this book to be maximized to its full potential, you must take it seriously. It really is a matter of life and death! I have written this book to overcome the premise of Albert Sweitzer, "the tragedy in life is what dies in a man while he is still alive." We have all had dreams die within us. They do not have to stay dead. We have the power to resurrect those dreams. It is time for us to wake up, and, more specifically, wake up our dreams! Let's bring to life those things (dreams, goals, etc.) that are dead.

By following the 42-day journey in this book, you will be on your way to changing the way you think and act; however, you must remember, although you are the one who will ultimately make the decision to change your life, you must also have a network of people who will be your cheerleading squad, as well as your coaching staff. (Cheerleaders keep us pepped up while coaches sometimes "chew" us out.) You <u>will</u> need the accountability! The Proverb says, "Plans fail for lack of counsel, but with many advisers they succeed" (Proverbs 15:22). Wise counsel is vitally importan* in the "No X-Cuses!" program. "As iron sharpens iron, so one person sharpens another." (Proverbs 27:17)

My accountability partners include some diverse individuals. One is a no-nonsense, straight up, take-it-or-leave it, kind of guy. He speaks the truth very blatantly. I never, ever have to wonder what he is thinking. I have others who, very compassionately, state the truth. However, their focus is on how the message is delivered. Then, I have one who is exceptionally gifted in listening. This person can have a whole conversation and never say a word. She allows me to just vent. Everyone needs these various kinds of individuals as their accountability partners.

In church history, accountability was extremely stressed during the early stages of the weekly meetings. They asked each other such questions as, "How is it with your soul?", and "In what ways have you sinned?" Even in the 1700's these people recognized the importance and strength that accountability posed. Perhaps the greatest thing they did was to verbalize the things that they would be working on (spiritually) during the upcoming week. This group made it a strong point to assure that these things would be accomplished.

The next 42-days is about stretching you and structuring your life in such a way to maximize your potential. You must have wise counsel in order to accomplish this. Please take time to fill out the covenant with your "accountability partners." Doing so may secure you living the "No X-Cuses!" lifestyle.

ACCOUNTABILITY COVENANT

I, _____, am entering a 42-day "No X-Cuses!" period in my life. For the next 42 days, I promise to do my daily reading, journal entry, and follow-ups. I am asking that the undersigned would lovingly accept only the best from me. I am promising for the next 42 days to have absolutely "No X-Cuses!," only results. By signing this covenant, you, the under signers, are promising to give me the love and support needed in order for me to reach my goals. By signing this, we are entering a covenant in which I am promising to live a new lifestyle and you are promising to hold me accountable to this new lifestyle. Your commitment to me will be to <u>daily</u> follow-up on my progress. Please love me enough to do this for me.

Sincerely,

_____
(name)

_____
(Accountability Partner)

_____
(Accountability Partner)

GOAL LIST

A couple of years ago, I was blessed to hear Reed DeVries speak. Reed spoke on the importance of having goals. His emphasis went even further than just having goals. "If one is to accomplish his goals, then he must write them down," said Reed. This is a concept that Brian Tracy refers to as "thinking on paper." I had heard that statement hundreds of times before. This time it took root. It was one of those "Ah, hah!" moments, an epiphany of sorts. Reed encouraged people to write 100 goals they wanted to accomplish before they died. I did just that. I started with 100, but, before long, my goal list had grown to about 116 goals.

Another part of Reed's exercise was for us to look at that goal list three times per day. I began looking at my list during breakfast, lunch, and supper (I am from the South, and we call it supper, not dinner). This little process started changing the way I think. I began to think about how I could make these goals become a reality.

A local newspaper heard about my list. They asked if they could do a local interest story on me. Being a person who is not bashful, I naturally agreed. The story sparked an inordinate amount of interest from people in the community. I did not, and still do not, consider my story unique. However, I have discovered that it is different. Sociologists will agree that most people (98%) will never write down their goals. Out of this group, fewer than two percent will actually accomplish those goals. Now, I realize how unusual it is to have an active goal list.

How did this process change my life? For one thing, I began to look for opportunities to accomplish my goals. As a byproduct, I became empowered. At the time, my greatest fear was high altitudes. Even though I flew quite often, I always tried to keep the thought of the high altitude out of my mind. Because of the goal list, I have overcome that fear.

It happened on a beautiful October day in 2003. I climbed on board of an old, crusty-looking airplane and began the flight upward. However, on that day, things would be different. Instead of landing with the plane, I would be taking a different path. One of my goals was to go skydiving. It was one of the most incredible things I have ever done! On that day, I overcame a fear and accomplished a goal, all thanks to my list.

I encourage you to make a list of 100 things you want to accomplish before you die. After you have developed that list, look at it three times a day. Your life will hinge on accomplishing these goals. The feelings you receive while completing these things will be indescribable.

During the next 42 days, develop a list of both short-term and long-term goals you WILL accomplish. This list is vitally important. You will need to refer to this list on a daily basis. Make a list of goals (at least 2 for the next six weeks) that addresses each aspect of the triangle of wholeness: the spiritual, the physical, and the mental/emotional. This list should not be a "pie in the sky" list. This should be a practical list that causes **focused intentionality**. Do you want to lose weight during this time? Do you want to increase your salary? Whatever the goal, put it on that list. After you have mapped out that list, then you will need a game plan to make those things come true. On the page that follows, write a list of at least 6 things you want to accomplish and the way you intend to do it. I also encourage you to list the challenges you will need to overcome in order to be successful in your quest. State the goal and list the three action steps you will need to do to accomplish this goal. Under each action step, list the 3 obstacles you will have to overcome to accomplish this action. Your decisions will change your life. Many people place too much emphasis on the accomplish date itself. While this date is important, it can change. Please do not accept defeat just because the goal date may have to be pushed back. Life happens. This activity is about the process of becoming a better person, not being obsessed about a certain date. I can put this into personal terminology. I once made a goal of running a marathon. The completion date was April 26th. The last day before the marathon I knew that I was not physically ready for the race. I had to pick a new date and run a later marathon. Was I a failure? No. Life dealt some things that made me restructure my goals. In the process, I learned patience.

The Triangle of Wholeness

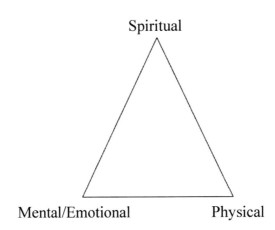

Spiritual

Mental/Emotional   Physical

One example of my spiritual goals is follows:

Goal #1: To increase my focus and time to the reading of Scripture.

Action Step #1: Wake up Early (Do My Reading during the morning time)

Obstacle #1: Go to Bed Earlier

Obstacle#2: Eliminate the Use of the Snooze Button on the alarm clock

Obstacle#3: Exercise in the Morning (Stimulates my thinking)

Goal Sheet

List Your Goal, the date to accomplish the goal, the action step that you must take, and the obstacles that must be overcome in order to accomplish your goal.

"A dream is just a dream. A goal is a dream with a plan and a deadline."—Harvey Mackay

Goal #1

_____

_____**Date**_____

Action Step #1_____

Obstacle #1

_____

_____

Obstacle #2

_____

_____

Obstacle #3

_____

_____

Action Step #2_____

Obstacle #1
_____
_____

Obstacle #2
_____
_____

Obstacle #3
_____
_____

Action Step #3
_____
_____

Obstacle #1
_____
_____

Obstacle #2
_____
_____

Obstacle #3
_____
_____

Goal #2 _____

_____**Date**_____

Action Step #1
_____
_____

Obstacle #1

_____

_____

Obstacle #2

_____

_____

Obstacle #3

_____

_____

Action Step #2

_____

_____

Obstacle #1

_____

_____

Obstacle #2

_____

_____

Obstacle #3

_____

_____

Action Step #3

_____

_____

Obstacle #1

_____

_____

Obstacle #2

_____
_____

Obstacle #3

_____
_____

Goal #3 _____

_____**Date**_____

Action Step #1

_____
_____

Obstacle #1

_____
_____

Obstacle #2

_____
_____

Obstacle #3

_____
_____

Action Step #2

_____
_____

Obstacle #1

_____
_____

Obstacle #2

_____

_____

Obstacle #3

_____

_____

Action Step #3

_____

_____

Obstacle #1

_____

_____

Obstacle #2

_____

_____

Obstacle #3

_____

_____

Goal #4 _____

_____**Date**_____

Action Step #1

Obstacle #1

_____

_____

Obstacle #2

_____

_____

Obstacle #3

_____

_____

Action Step #2

_____

_____

Obstacle #1

_____

_____

Obstacle #2

_____

_____

Obstacle #3

_____

_____

Action Step #3

_____

_____

Obstacle #1

_____

_____

Obstacle #2

_____

_____

Obstacle #3

_____

_____

No X-Cuses!

Goal #5 _____

_____**Date**_____

Action Step #1
_____
_____

Obstacle #1
_____
_____

Obstacle #2
_____
_____

Obstacle #3
_____
_____

Action Step #2
_____
_____

Obstacle #1
_____
_____

Obstacle #2
_____
_____

Obstacle #3
_____
_____

Action Step #3

_____
_____

Obstacle #1

_____
_____

Obstacle #2

_____
_____

Obstacle #3

_____
_____

Goal #6 _____

_____**Date**_____

Action Step #1

_____
_____

Obstacle #1

_____
_____

Obstacle #2

_____
_____

Obstacle #3

_____
_____

Action Step #2

_____

_____

Obstacle #1

_____

_____

Obstacle #2

_____

_____

Obstacle #3

_____

_____

Action Step #3

_____

_____

Obstacle #1

_____

_____

Obstacle #2

_____

_____

Obstacle #3

_____

_____

DAILY READING AND JOURNAL

Dr. Norman Vincent Peale once said, "Change your thoughts, and you change your world." Daily reading and journaling are an integral part of the change process. Expand your mind by expanding the subjects that you read. The daily readings are meant to be an "eye-opening" experience. Your thought process should be engaged to changing a specific part of your life.

Reading is only the first part of the process. I encourage these readings to be done in the morning time, while the mind is still fresh. This will allow you to focus your day. More importantly, you will happen to your day instead of your day happening to you. This simple process will help you become more proactive about your life. By doing this, you will give yourself permission to succeed. This process will keep you centered on how you will live each day in such a way in order to accomplish your goals.

Journaling is the process of putting your new thought process onto paper. These words help us to understand ourselves better. "An unexamined life in not worth living" is a quote attributed to Socrates. Journaling gives each of us an opportunity to be honest with ourselves and to carefully examine our lives.

I encourage you to journal on things which come to mind. According to Les Brown, every year we have three to four thoughts, which, if only acted upon, would change our life. Write them down and expound on them. After all, we are supposed to be "loving God with our mind." By doing this one thing, we will allow God a new avenue into our lives to create miracles for ourselves and others.

Your journal is yours. These are words that only you will see. Unless you allow someone else that exclusive right, your words and thoughts will remain private.

It is very important during these exercises that you are completely honest with yourself. It may hurt! Change and growth do hurt. You are guaranteed to experience growing pains. Are you willing to do what it takes to change? It is up to you. In my office, I have a saying by Harry Browne which says, "You are where you are today because you have chosen to be there." You will also be where you are tomorrow because of the decisions you will make today. You are in control of those decisions!

THE THREE COMPONENTS
OF LIFE:

SPIRITUAL, PHYSICAL,
AND MENTAL/EMOTIONAL

It is my belief that the human being is comprised of three distinct parts: the physical, the mental/emotional, and the spiritual. If, at any time, one of these elements becomes out of balance, then the sum total of the human being is out of balance. Because of this belief, I have included a daily checklist to help insure these elements are being addressed. These elements are broken down into smaller categories in order to provide better focus in these areas.

The physical area of your life includes all those areas pertaining to how you treat your body. How much do you exercise? What are your eating habits? Do you eat a balanced diet? Are you taking vitamins and supplements? Are you drinking enough water? Julia Child said, "Water is the most neglected nutrient in your diet, but one of the most vital." How much sleep do you get? You cannot be the best unless you are giving your body the best advantage it can have.

Our society today tends to side step the importance of our spirituality. We will address it head on. The spiritual area includes your spiritual reading, Bible reading, and prayer time. Teilhard

DeChardin says, "We are not a human being having a spiritual experience. We are a spiritual being having a human experience." It is not my intention to proselytize you into my faith. It is my goal to have you recognize and embrace the spiritual dynamic of life. I encourage you to pray every day. By keeping a prayer journal, you may be able to stay better focused during your prayer time. Please remember, prayer is not only what you say to God, but also what God may say to you. Listen intently.

The last aspect to being completely healthy is the mental/emotional. Les Brown is quoted as saying, "Eighty-seven percent of our mind talk is negative." What books are you reading? How much time do you read every day? How much time do you spend in quiet/reflection time? What kind of positive feedback do you give to others? You cannot give to others without being changed yourself. Do you listen to positive CD's? Are you spending too much time watching television? These activities feed our brain, which, in turn will speak to us. GIGO is a computer term which says, "Garbage in, garbage out." What we put into our minds is what we end up thinking about. It is so important to be tuned into what we are feeding our brain.

In all of these areas, "positive" is the key word. We are striving for the "No X-Cuses!" lifestyle. We need all the positive influences we can get. By receiving the positive, then we are able to share the positive, thus we will be able to change the world. In order to live the "No X-Cuses!" lifestyle, you will need to faithfully address all these aspects in your life. I believe Ghandi said it best, "Be the change you want to see in the world." The power to choose a different life is in the power of your hands. What will you choose?

THE NEXT 42 DAYS

Two Roads diverged in a wood and I—
I took the one less traveled by,
And that has made all the difference.

from "The Road Not Taken" by Robert Frost

FRUSTRATIONS

"Our ultimate freedom is the right and power to decide
how anybody or anything outside ourselves will affect
us."—Stephen R. Covey

My brother died of complications from alcoholism. It is a terrible way to watch a person die. The process took several years, culminating in a week-long stay in a hospital in which he was kept alive using life-support machines. The final week ravaged his body to the point of utter chaos. I will never be able to describe the feeling as I watched his kidneys fail which caused the urine bag to fill with blood. I was helpless and hopeless. Thankfully, he had caring doctors and staff. After a week of watching his health decline so rapidly, we decided it was time to take him off of life support. After that decision, my brother, Michael, lived for one hour. His life ended way too soon. He was only forty eight years old.

Is alcoholism a disease or a choice? This is a debate that has intensified over the years. I fall somewhere in between. After dealing with Michael, I know it is a disease. On the other hand, every time Michael took a drink, he made the choice to die young. He knew what he could accomplish. He completed a six month rehabilitation program, a time during which his body almost completely rejuvenated itself. His liver was healthier than it had been in years. At that point, I had faith that he had overcome his demons. I was wrong.

Alcoholism is a family disease. The addict is not the only one affected by his/her addiction. The turmoil caused by this beast is pure insanity. Overall, there is very little guidance to help families deal with the daily insanity that is thrust into their lives. The question I hear addicts' families ask all the time is, "Where do we go when there seems like no hope?" That is a question for which I still struggle for the answer.

I have come to realize that one cannot rationalize with an irrational person. During my brother's addiction, I begged him many times to stop drinking. There are so many things I wished I would have said. Many times, I said the wrong thing. Words hurt whether you are sober or intoxicated. I have many regrets over the words and the tone that I used to talk to my brother. Words said in frustration cannot ever be taken back. I said some cruel things to him disguised as tough love, which in reality, was just a way in which I could rid myself of the frustration of losing control.

Michael was sober for over eight months. For some reason, which nobody knows, he began to drink again. After deciding to drink again, he drank with a vengeance. It was almost, as if, he had to make up for lost time. Because of the intensity of his drinking, Michael spent the better part of a year in and out of the hospital. After his death, we threw away over thirty empty whiskey bottles that were left in his room. Literally, his life had been reduced to eating, drinking alcohol, and sleeping. A terrible waste for such a talented person.

I began writing this book in 2007. Until May 2011, I still did not have a clear focus as to why I was writing it. During one of the small groups that I teach, one of the participants asked me a pointed question, "Mark, why do you teach this stuff?" I finally knew the answer. Jesus once asked a paralytic man a simple, but complex question. He asked him, "Do you want to get well?" Paraphrased he asked him, "Do you want to get better?" (John 5) I have written this book to help people get better! No matter what you are going through, you can get better. You really can live your life fully in all aspects: spiritually, physically, and mentally/emotionally.

"Where there is life there is hope." This mantra can be your life's motto. Even in the middle of your life's struggles, how can you "take back" your life? Everyone has greatness inside of them. Your greatness is bigger than any of your difficulties!

I am especially sensitive to those dealing with the issue of addictions. The insanity of dealing with addictions will take its toll, even with the best of us. From my experience, I learned that in any situation, I ask myself, "How can I better deal with those around me?" Where do you go when there seems to be no hope? How do you handle things when you are not "in control?" How does this relate to your spiritual, physical, and mental/emotional aspects of your life?

Date_____

NO X-CUSES!

Journal

"What I am looking for is not out there, it is in me."
—Helen Keller

_____
_____
_____
_____
_____
_____
_____
_____
_____
_____
_____
_____
_____
_____
_____
_____
_____
_____
_____
_____
_____
_____
_____
_____
_____
_____
_____
_____

Date_____

NO X-CUSES!

Physical

Did you exercise today? ☐ yes ☐ no

What exercise did you do?

Did you eat healthy today? ☐ yes ☐ no

Did you get enough sleep? ☐ yes ☐ no

Did you drink enough water? ☐ yes ☐ no

Did you take your vitamins/supplements? ☐ yes ☐ no

Spiritual

Did you do your Bible reading today? ☐ yes ☐ no

What did you read?

Did you pray today? ☐ yes ☐ no

What did you pray about?

How much quiet time did you spend today?

Mental/Emotional

What positive books/magazines did you read?

Did you spend personal thought-time today? ☐ yes ☐ no

What positive words did you speak to others?

What positive CDs did you listen to?

HEALTH

"Success is a journey, not a destination. The doing is often
more important than the outcome."
—Arthur Ashe

Health is a big thing these days. It seems there is a big push to live stronger, healthier lives all the while the obesity rate in our nation continues to rise. A healthy lifestyle is comprised of many aspects: exercise, proper amount of sleep, good nutrition, lack of stress, good network of support from friends, and attention to the spiritual needs of your life. These components must be addressed if one is to live a full and successful life.

Health is a vital component of the No X-Cuses! program. One cannot be completely whole without being completely physically healthy. There is something between the exercise/health connection with your mental/emotional and spiritual components that cannot be overlooked. We are whole and complete beings, and we must address life as such. We cannot and will not be whole and successful until we take care of our physical health.

I make no apologies for my beliefs on the effects of exercise. In the past, I have had weight struggles for most of my life. When I allow my weight to get out of control, I have numerous health problems, the greatest of which is extremely high blood pressure. I have seen times in my life when my blood pressure was 240/140. I was a walking stroke.

Heart attacks run in my family genes. My father died at the age of 52 of a massive heart attack. It probably could have been avoided. He was overweight, did not exercise, he smoked, and he chewed tobacco. These things had to precipitate to his demise. I refuse to allow these family genes to get to me! My favorite saying, "They may be my genes (jeans), but I don't have to wear them."

I have taken charge of my life. First and foremost, I have a great health care provider, Bonnie Judd, BA, BSN, MSN, APN and certified FNP. She is very sensitive and caring, regarding my health care. Hopefully, all practitioners are the same. Her "calling" is medicine and everyone can tell it. She keeps a major check on everything for me. In order to live as positive a lifestyle as possible, one must have a primary care provider that does the same.

The most important thing is that I am the one who is responsible for my health! It is my body, so I have been entrusted by God, to take care of it to the best of my ability, with no excuses accepted!

How does that look for me? How do I maintain the best physical health possible for myself? Do I get regular physical checkups? Do I maintain a proper nutritional diet? Do I exercise at least thirty minutes for three times per week?

Date_____

NO X-CUSES!

Journal

"The most important ability is . . . . responsibility"
—Dr. John Maxwell

_____
_____
_____
_____
_____
_____
_____
_____
_____
_____
_____
_____
_____
_____
_____
_____
_____
_____
_____
_____
_____
_____
_____
_____
_____
_____
_____
_____
_____
_____
_____
_____

Date_____

NO X-CUSES!

<u>Physical</u>

Did you exercise today? ☐ yes ☐ no

What exercise did you do?

Did you eat healthy today? ☐ yes ☐ no

Did you get enough sleep? ☐ yes ☐ no

Did you drink enough water? ☐ yes ☐ no

Did you take your vitamins/supplements? ☐ yes ☐ no

<u>Spiritual</u>

Did you do your Bible reading today? ☐ yes ☐ no

What did you read?

Did you pray today? ☐ yes ☐ no

What did you pray about?

Mental/Emotional

What positive books/magazines did you read?

Did you spend personal thought-time today? ☐ yes ☐ no

What positive words did you speak to others?

What positive CDs did you listen to?

START SMALL, BUILD BIG

"I don't believe in circumstances. The people who get on in this
world are the people who get up and look for the circumstances
they want, and, if they can't find them, make them."
-George Bernard Shaw

Being out of shape, I knew I needed to change. I knew it was time to choose to get in better shape. The old adage is, "You eat an elephant one bite at a time." Getting back into shape would take me the same kind of mentality. I would have to start small and build big.

I often hear people say things like, "I have always been big," or "being fat runs in my family." Those statements make me cringe. I find similar statements to be excuses for people to remain in unhealthy lifestyles. Those statements give people the hopelessness they will need to continue losing in life.

My family heritage contains overweight people who never took care of themselves. They blame their obesity on our family tree. As harsh as it sounds, it is not my grandfather or grandmother's fault if I choose to be fat. God has given me the freewill to choose whether or not if I am going to exercise and eat healthily.

When I was overweight, I made the decision to get healthy and back into strong physical health. It did not take me a week to get a hundred pounds overweight, and it did not take me a week to get back into shape. I reasoned that I must be patient and give the process some time. So, I started where I was. I began to do one push-up and one sit-up every morning and evening. Each week, I increased it one extra in the morning and one extra in the evening. At this point in my life, I start and end everyday by doing fifty push-ups and fifty sit-ups.

The same process began to take shape with my cardio routine. I began my running routine by walking only five minutes on the treadmill. My first mile walking took me twenty minutes to complete, but I did not stop. As of today, I have run two marathons and am training for my first triathlon. Has it been easy? No. Nothing in life that is worthwhile rarely is easy. I am happy to say that I have run thirty three miles without stopping. I faithfully ride my bicycle twenty to thirty miles at least three times a week. As you read this, I weigh in at 207 pounds, a one hundred pound weight loss from my previous weight. I have done things that I once thought were impossible. Just think, this whole process started out with one push-up and one sit-up.

What major things do you want to accomplish? How can you start small and build large? Looking at the things you wish to accomplish in life, what can you do to start out small? How can this be applied to the major areas of your life: the physical, spiritual, and mental/ emotional?

Wherever you are in life, start and then trust the process.

Date_____

NO X-CUSES!

Journal

"The man who moved a mountain was the one who began
carrying away small stones"
—Chinese Proverb

_____
_____
_____
_____
_____
_____
_____
_____
_____
_____
_____
_____
_____
_____
_____
_____
_____
_____
_____
_____
_____
_____
_____
_____
_____
_____
_____
_____
_____
_____

Date_____

NO X-CUSES!

Physical

Did you exercise today? ☐ yes ☐ no

What exercise did you do?

Did you eat healthy today? ☐ yes ☐ no

Did you get enough sleep? ☐ yes ☐ no

Did you drink enough water? ☐ yes ☐ no

Did you take your vitamins/supplements? ☐ yes ☐ no

Spiritual

Did you do your Bible reading today? ☐ yes ☐ no

What did you read?

Did you pray today? ☐ yes ☐ no

What did you pray about?

Mental/Emotional

What positive books/magazines did you read?

Did you spend personal thought-time today? ☐ yes ☐ no

What positive words did you speak to others?

What positive CDs did you listen to?

Day 4

HELPING OTHERS

The less you open your heart to others, the more your heart
suffers.
—Deepak Chopra

I conduct many small group goal classes. During these classes, I often have the participants do many different group exercises together. As a leader, I never really know what results will happen. Often times, the personalities of the participants cause a different response from the one I had intended to happen.

During one of my small groups something unexpected happened. We were participating in an activity in which one participant was blindfolded, turned around and then expected to throw a ball into a trash can. It is an exercise intended to prove how difficult it is for us to hit a goal which we cannot see. This particular occasion taught me another invaluable lesson.

As I blindfolded the participant, I turned her around. She had no idea which direction the goal was. As she was stumbling throughout the room, her husband opted not to help her and jumped out of her way. In spite of all this, one person in the group took her by the hand and led her to the goal. As he did that, another man in the group picked up the garbage can which helped her to make the goal.

This process showed me how important it is to help others. Many people will never be able to hit their goals and dreams without your help. This does not have to be a grand process either. There are always small things we can do to help others. Albert Schweitzer said it best when he said, "Wherever you turn, you can find someone who needs you. Even if it is a little thing, do something for which there is no pay but the privilege of doing it. Remember, you don't live in a world all of your own." There is only one way to really reach our goals and that is to look for ways to help other people.

What can you do to help others reach their goals? Who can you think of right now that can use your help to reach a specific goal? What resources, talents, or time can you give another that would step them closer to success in their lives? Who needs help? How can you help?

> "You can get everything you want in life, as long as you help enough other people get what they want, without ever wanting anything in return."—Zig Ziglar

Date_____

NO X-CUSES!

Journal

"Behind an able man there are always other able men."
Chinese proverb

_____
_____
_____
_____
_____
_____
_____
_____
_____
_____
_____
_____
_____
_____
_____
_____
_____
_____
_____
_____
_____
_____
_____
_____
_____
_____
_____
_____
_____
_____
_____

Date_____

NO X-CUSES!

Physical

Did you exercise today? ☐ yes ☐ no

What exercise did you do?

Did you eat healthy today? ☐ yes ☐ no

Did you get enough sleep? ☐ yes ☐ no

Did you drink enough water? ☐ yes ☐ no

Did you take your vitamins/supplements? ☐ yes ☐ no

Spiritual

Did you do your Bible reading today? ☐ yes ☐ no

What did you read?

Did you pray today? ☐ yes ☐ no

What did you pray about?

Mental/Emotional

What positive books/magazines did you read?

Did you spend personal thought-time today? ☐ yes ☐ no

What positive words did you speak to others?

What positive CDs did you listen to?

LIVING BY EXAMPLE

"Example is not the main thing in influencing others. It is the
only thing."
—Albert Schweitzer

At the tender age of 6, I picked up a nasty habit. Gratefully, the habit was short-lived. As a matter of fact, the habit lasted only one cigarette. My habit came to an end because of a "rat-fink" sister (I really love my sister; however, I have to use descriptive terms for dramatic purposes).

I had stolen one of my dad's cigarettes. With the intention of sneaking around the back of the house, I was going to enjoy my first puff of the "heavenly nicotine." The real outcome was far from my expectations. Thanks to my sister, I had an unwelcome guest, my dad, who quickly snatched that cigarette right out of my mouth. The audacity of that man! I could tell he was angry because he kept grinding his back teeth.

As he pulled the cigarette out of my mouth, I responded in a sarcastic tone, "You smoke!" The inconsistency of his answer still echoes with me today. "You do as I say, not as I do." Even as a 6-year old boy, I thought that to be a very odd statement. How could he expect me to live by a standard that he did not live by? After the ensuing butt-whipping (my parents did not believe in "time out"), I was "cured" of my desire for nicotine.

Being 42 years old, this is one of my experiences that has never been forgotten. I have often considered the irony of this circumstance. My dad, who had smoked the majority of his life, somehow felt his words were more powerful than his example. As a young child, I understood the power of action and example. However, as adults, we want to diminish that power. We often call politicians and pastors "hypocrites" for doing things that they oppose. Could it be that we practice the same form of hypocrisy? We expect others to follow our words without giving prudence to our actions. How stupid is that?

Let us live our lives in such a way that there is no difference between our words and our actions.

ADDRESSING THE SPIRITUAL, PHYSICAL, AND MENTAL/EMOTIONAL:

What standards do you set? Do you live by them? What can you do to set a better standard? Are you physically fit? What spiritual standards are you living by? Do you expect others to live by a standard you are not living by? Do you have inconsistencies that cause you mental stress? How do you emotionally handle those inconsistencies? How can you choose to overcome those inconsistencies?

Date_____

NO X-CUSES!

Journal

"People of double standards never experience happiness."
—Sam Veda

_____
_____
_____
_____
_____
_____
_____
_____
_____
_____
_____
_____
_____
_____
_____
_____
_____
_____
_____
_____
_____
_____
_____
_____
_____
_____
_____
_____
_____
_____

Date_____

NO X-CUSES!

Physical

Did you exercise today? ☐ yes ☐ no

What exercise did you do?

Did you eat healthy today? ☐ yes ☐ no

Did you get enough sleep? ☐ yes ☐ no

Did you drink enough water? ☐ yes ☐ no

Did you take your vitamins/supplements? ☐ yes ☐ no

Spiritual

Did you do your Bible reading today? ☐ yes ☐ no

What did you read?

Did you pray today? ☐ yes ☐ no

What did you pray about?

Mental/Emotional

What positive books/magazines did you read?

Did you spend personal thought-time today? ☐ yes ☐ no

What positive words did you speak to others?

What positive CDs did you listen to?

Day 6

CHANGING YOUR LIFE

"It is in our moments of decision that our destiny is shaped."
—Anthony Robbins

New Year's Eve 2001 was a monumental time in my life. Overall, my life was not heading in the direction in which I wanted. My professional career was stagnant and my weight had ballooned to over 300 pounds. With my family history (my dad died at fifty-two with a massive heart attack and my brother had a heart attack at age forty), I was a heart attack waiting to happen.

New Year's Eve found me lying in bed just staring at the ceiling. I remember asking, "Am I going to lie to myself again or am I going to live this year differently?" That night, I made a promise to myself and to God that I was going to lose weight. Even though I had made the commitment, it took me three more weeks to join the gym.

Choosing to live differently, I lost eighty-three pounds. That year, in December, I ran my first marathon. Accomplishing my goals, I had a new standard of living. For the first time, I felt empowered to accomplish almost anything.

That decision caused me to eventually live life differently. First and foremost, I decided that I had to change my diet. That was pretty easy to do. When I enter a restaurant, I see what fat people are eating, and I order something else. The statement may seem harsh, but it is a guideline that I have used to keep myself healthy. Secondly, I have to exercise daily. Exercise does two things for me. It provides me a way to stay physically healthy, but it also gives me the time to focus my mind. I have also found that I do not pay the price for exercise. I enjoy the benefits. My life is better because of the decision to live differently that the "average" person.

Is this easy? No. I am often tempted to not exercise or to eat unhealthily. Do I always act as a disciplined person? No. It is the routine of examining my decisions and evaluating my life that causes me to make fewer and fewer unhealthy choices. Making one great decision empowers me to make another one. Great choices produce more great choices.

ADDRESSING THE SPIRITUAL, PHYSICAL, AND MENTAL/EMOTIONAL:

For me, I made the decision on New Year's Eve, but it took me three more weeks to begin to put it into practice. Are there decisions you have made but never acted upon? What will it take in order for you to follow-up on your decision? What decisions can you make and put into action to change your life spiritually, physically, and mentally/emotionally? Do you really want to change? Are you settling for mediocrity?

Date_____

NO X-CUSES!

Journal

"Remember, a real decision is measured by the fact that you've taken new action. If there's no action, you haven't truly decided."
—Anthony Robbins

_____
_____
_____
_____
_____
_____
_____
_____
_____
_____
_____
_____
_____
_____
_____
_____
_____
_____
_____
_____
_____
_____
_____
_____
_____
_____
_____
_____

Date_____

NO X-CUSES!

Physical

Did you exercise today? ☐ yes ☐ no

What exercise did you do?

Did you eat healthy today? ☐ yes ☐ no

Did you get enough sleep? ☐ yes ☐ no

Did you drink enough water? ☐ yes ☐ no

Did you take your vitamins/supplements? ☐ yes ☐ no

Spiritual

Did you do your Bible reading today? ☐ yes ☐ no

What did you read?

Did you pray today? ☐ yes ☐ no

What did you pray about?

Mental/Emotional

What positive books/magazines did you read?

Did you spend personal thought-time today? ☐ yes ☐ no

What positive words did you speak to others?

What positive CDs did you listen to?

TOUGH TIMES WILL COME

"It's not the will to win that matters—everyone has that. It's
the will to prepare to win that matters."
—Coach Paul "Bear" Bryant

During 2002, I fell in love with the sport of running. It proved to be my vehicle for continued weight loss. My passion for running was so intense; I decided I was going to run a marathon. At the time of this decision, I still weighed in excess of 250 pounds. It was a lofty goal for me considering I had problems walking from the recliner to the refrigerator, which was a trip I often took.

In order for this goal to become a reality, I had to take an inventory of myself. One thing I knew well about myself: I am the king of making excuses. Having made losing weight such an important goal for me, I knew I would have to take away any possibility for excuses. Preparations had to be made. I had to list my action steps and then know which obstacles I would have to overcome in order to reach my goals.

Anyone can run when the weather is perfect; however, it takes a special breed to run when it is cold and rainy. I knew this would be my challenge. If I were to accomplish my goal of running a marathon, then I might have to run in rain and inclement weather. My greatest challenge would come when I needed to run; however, the weather would not be cooperating.

To avoid excuses, I began the preparation process. I went to my favorite running store and made a three hundred dollar investment and bought a Gore-Tex waterproof running suit. The investment cemented my determination to accomplish this feat. I knew the rain would come, and I would have to be ready for it. This also cemented one more important fact about myself. I go where my money goes. If I invest monetarily, then I am emotionally bonded to my goal.

ADDRESSING THE SPIRITUAL, PHYSICAL, AND MENTAL/EMOTIONAL:

It is not a question whether the tough times will come. The real question is, "When are the tough times coming?" What tough times are looming for you ahead? Are you ready for the challenge? Are you preparing for the tough times? What investment are you making to insure you will survive the tumultuous times?

> "The time to repair the roof is when the sun is shining."—John F. Kennedy

Date_____

NO X-CUSES!

Journal

"Success always comes when preparation meets opportunity."
—Henry Hartman

_____

_____

_____

_____

_____

_____

_____

_____

_____

_____

_____

_____

_____

_____

_____

_____

_____

_____

_____

_____

_____

_____

_____

_____

_____

_____

_____

_____

_____

_____

_____

Date_____

NO X-CUSES!

Physical

Did you exercise today? ☐ yes ☐ no

What exercise did you do?

Did you eat healthy today? ☐ yes ☐ no

Did you get enough sleep? ☐ yes ☐ no

Did you drink enough water? ☐ yes ☐ no

Did you take your vitamins/supplements? ☐ yes ☐ no

Spiritual

Did you do your Bible reading today? ☐ yes ☐ no

What did you read?

Did you pray today? ☐ yes ☐ no

What did you pray about?

Mental/Emotional

What positive books/magazines did you read?

Did you spend personal thought-time today? ☐ yes ☐ no

What positive words did you speak to others?

What positive CDs did you listen to?

GRABBING THE THROTTLE

"Grab the bull by the horns. It makes for one indescribable
ride!"
—Mark Beecham

What holds you back from going "all out" for your dreams? Is it family, friends, or your own fears and insecurities? Failure is tough to live with. How about living with the regret of not doing what you wanted to do? Live life with boldness and risk more.

My nephews are the most important people in my life. They have taught me many valuable lessons about life. Through them, I have learned how to enjoy the "small things" in life. Today, my nephews are growing up into mature young men. They make me very proud to be their uncle.

My younger nephew, Chandler, taught me about how he handles life. A few years ago when he was only six years old, I took him riding on my jet ski. After getting him on the craft and latching the key onto my life jacket (a smart decision on my part), I started the jet ski. As I looked to say something to the people on the dock, Chandler reached up and grabbed the throttle as hard as he could.

Although I almost flipped off the craft, I finally regained my balance. Meanwhile, I looked up and saw the brightest smile on Chandler's face. I could not even begin to describe his laugh. He loves to live life at full throttle. I wished I had more of this characteristic in my own life. I wished I could "cut loose" and let it all hang out.

Through that process, I have discovered the five rules that allow one to really grab life "by the horns":

1) Decide what you want.

2) Write it down.

3) "Tunnel Vision" your goal. Make your goal your focal point.

4) Surround yourself with people who support you and your goal.

5) Go with it with ALL your focus and energy.

ADDRESSING THE SPIRITUAL, PHYSICAL, AND MENTAL/EMOTIONAL:

How could you change your life spiritually, physically, and mentally/emotionally that would allow you to live it "all out"? Are there areas in your life where you could just go for it? What is holding you back from going all out for your dreams? Could you surround yourself with enthusiastic people who could help you grab the gusto for life? Who are they?

Date_____

NO X-CUSES!

Journal

"I am more and more convinced that our happiness or
unhappiness depends more on the way we meet the events of
life than on the nature of those events themselves."
—Alexander Humboldt

_____
_____
_____
_____
_____
_____
_____
_____
_____
_____
_____
_____
_____
_____
_____
_____
_____
_____
_____
_____
_____
_____
_____
_____
_____
_____
_____
_____
_____
_____

Date_____

NO X-CUSES!

Physical

Did you exercise today? ☐ yes ☐ no

What exercise did you do?

Did you eat healthy today? ☐ yes ☐ no

Did you get enough sleep? ☐ yes ☐ no

Did you drink enough water? ☐ yes ☐ no

Did you take your vitamins/supplements? ☐ yes ☐ no

Spiritual

Did you do your Bible reading today? ☐ yes ☐ no

What did you read?

Did you pray today? ☐ yes ☐ no

What did you pray about?

Mental/Emotional

What positive books/magazines did you read?

Did you spend personal thought-time today? ☐ yes ☐ no

What positive words did you speak to others?

What positive CDs did you listen to?

OVERCOMING OBSTACLES

"Opportunity Creates Desire."
—Danish Proverb

What is your most embarrassing moment? We all have them. We have those moments that we would like to forget. They may always be impressions in our minds; however, they do not define who we are.

As a group of my friends were sitting around one day, we began sharing our life's most embarrassing moment. We all had funny stories to share, although one story stood out. Gary took a chance and shared his story. Although we tried not to laugh, we all found ourselves laughing uncontrollably.

Gary was a great athlete. He attended a small college on a basketball scholarship. Because of his scholarship, he found himself playing against tough competition. Many of his competitors went on to play professional basketball. It was one of these competitors who provided Gary with his most embarrassing moment.

Back in the late 1980's, the University of Houston had an incredible basketball program. The stars on that team included Hakeem Olajuwan and Clyde "the Glide" Drexler. Some still contend they were the best college team ever. Whatever the case, they would dunk the ball over anybody at anytime.

Gary was 6'7" and played forward for his team. On one particular play, Gary was the only one back on defense. As he looked up, he saw Clyde "the Glide" Drexler coming at him at full speed. As Gary recounted the story, he said, "At that moment I made a decision he was not going to dunk over me no matter what I had to do." His efforts failed.

Clyde began his jump just inside the free throw line. As he began to rise, Gary grabbed him around the waist in order to prevent the dunk. Gary said the next thing he remembered was the ball hitting him in the head as it passed through the goal.

Many people would have let the obstacle get in their way from scoring the goal. Not Clyde "the Glide." As Clyde took off from the free throw line, he knew he was not going to allow Gary to keep him from scoring. What a lesson in tenacity!

People who accomplish their goals "no matter the cost" do 4 things:

1) They clearly see the goal

2) They recognize the obstacles

   -They do not give the obstacles power which they don't have

3) They decide on a game plan.

   -The know the action steps to overcome the obstacles.

4) They take action and begin immediately.

ADDRESSING THE SPIRITUAL, PHYSICAL, AND MENTAL/EMOTIONAL:

Do you allow obstacles to keep you from your goal? Are you satisfied falling short of your goal? What obstacles are between you and your goal today? What can you do to rise over these obstacles? What can you do to empower yourself spiritually, physically, and mentally/emotionally to overcome obstacles?

Date_____

NO X-CUSES!

Journal

"It still holds true that man is most uniquely human when he
turns obstacles into opportunities."
—Eric Hoffer

_____
_____
_____
_____
_____
_____
_____
_____
_____
_____
_____
_____
_____
_____
_____
_____
_____
_____
_____
_____
_____
_____
_____
_____
_____
_____
_____
_____
_____
_____
_____
_____

Date_____

NO X-CUSES!

Physical

Did you exercise today? ☐ yes ☐ no

What exercise did you do?

Did you eat healthy today? ☐ yes ☐ no

Did you get enough sleep? ☐ yes ☐ no

Did you drink enough water? ☐ yes ☐ no

Did you take your vitamins/supplements? ☐ yes ☐ no

Spiritual

Did you do your Bible reading today? ☐ yes ☐ no

What did you read?

Did you pray today? ☐ yes ☐ no

What did you pray about?

Mental/Emotional

What positive books/magazines did you read?

Did you spend personal thought-time today? ☐ yes ☐ no

What positive words did you speak to others?

What positive CDs did you listen to?

DECISIONS WE LIVE WITH

"Our lives are a sum total of the choices we have made."
—Dr. Wayne Dyer

You can choose your friends, but you are stuck with your relatives. I believe we all have relatives that are interesting, to say the very least. Fortunately or unfortunately, my family tree is lined with such characters. Jeff Foxworthy could get a lifetime of material from one of my family reunions.

Harris was an older cousin of mine. When I say older, I mean much older. Harris was in his late 60's when I was just eight years old. Despite the generation gap, I listened to what he said. Harris had a characteristic that mystified me: a wooden leg.

Being such a young, inquisitive boy, I was intrigued by the wooden leg. I often wondered why he had the leg, but I would never dare ask him. Many times, I would just stare at that leg. He had a hole about the size of a quarter in the lower part of the leg around his ankle. The hole seemed to always lure my attention.

Finally, I had to find out about that leg. While visiting Harris' home, I asked my dad about the leg. He directed me to ask Harris. To my amazement, Harris was willing to speak freely about the subject. I hung onto every word.

Harris was a "young buck" in his earlier days ("young buck" is a Southern term which means wild and carefree). It seems that during one of his wild spells he became inebriated (dog drunk). I cannot recall exactly how the accident happened. Harris just said that he ended up being run over by a train, thus severing his leg from the rest of his body.

The story was very graphic for an eight-year old boy. Although it has been a story I have never forgotten, it was the comment he made after the story that has forever struck in the recesses of my mind. He said, "It didn't hurt at the time, but it has hurt every day since." His bad decision lived with him every day for the rest of his life.

I have a quote on my board in my office which states, "I am today because of the decisions I made yesterday." While I do not know who made this quote, its simplicity is steeped in wisdom.

How does a person make good decisions?

1) Have a plan.

2) Every decision must revolve around making that plan come to fruition.

3) Accept failures made as opportunities for education and growth. (Failures are positive experiences if they allow us to get closer to our goals.)

ADDRESSING THE SPIRITUAL, PHYSICAL, AND MENTAL/EMOTIONAL:

Are there decisions you have made in the past that still haunt you today? How have those decisions affected your life? What lessons can you learn from those decisions? How can you share those lessons with other people?

Date_____

NO X-CUSES!

Journal

"I think that somehow, we learn who we really are and then
live with that decision."
—Eleanor Roosevelt

_____
_____
_____
_____
_____
_____
_____
_____
_____
_____
_____
_____
_____
_____
_____
_____
_____
_____
_____
_____
_____
_____
_____
_____
_____
_____
_____

Date_____

NO X-CUSES!

Physical

Did you exercise today? ☐ yes ☐ no

What exercise did you do?

Did you eat healthy today? ☐ yes ☐ no

Did you get enough sleep? ☐ yes ☐ no

Did you drink enough water? ☐ yes ☐ no

Did you take your vitamins/supplements? ☐ yes ☐ no

Spiritual

Did you do your Bible reading today? ☐ yes ☐ no

What did you read?

Did you pray today? ☐ yes ☐ no

What did you pray about?

Mental/Emotional

What positive books/magazines did you read?

Did you spend personal thought-time today? ☐ yes ☐ no

What positive words did you speak to others?

What positive CDs did you listen to?

FOCUSED INTENTIONALITY

"Concentrate all your thoughts upon the work at hand. The
sun's rays do not burn until brought to focus."
—Alexander Graham Bell

At the age of sixteen, my father died. A lose of that magnitude, at such a young age, is extremely traumatic. Being at such an impressionable age, I made a commitment to always make people and relationships a priority in my life. Due to that commitment, I choose to spend time with my friends and family over other possibilities.

On one of the many excursions that my friends and I have taken, we saw something that horrified us. Traveling not too far from my hometown, we were behind a tractor-trailer. To our amazement, the driver began to swerve back and forth, almost hitting cars passing by. After near misses, the driver swerved off the road and down a twenty-five foot embankment.

With diesel fuel gushing out of the capsized truck, another motorist and I climbed down the embankment. Without much effort, we were able to pull the driver out of the truck. Amazingly enough, the driver was uninjured. He had one knot on his forehead. A minor injury received for such a tremendous crash.

After further investigation, it became apparent the driver had fallen asleep. As many times as he had swerved into the other lane, it was a miracle he had not hurt a passing motorist. He had lost his focus, thus causing all of the chaos. This lack of focus could have cost him or someone else their lives.

There are practical ways for one to improve focus:

1) Take care of yourself physically. In order to maintain maximum effectiveness, one must take care of the body. In

the Book of Life, the body is referred to as "the temple." In order for the body to be at its peak performance, one must eat right and get enough sleep.

2) Take care of yourself spiritually. "Live the sermon you preach" is an old adage that I have heard most of my life. One cannot be in tune with themselves spiritually, if one is living counterproductive to their morals.

3) Take care of yourself mentally/emotionally. This could be the most difficult. One must surround themselves with things that only build up. With the wildfire of negativity within our society, one has to be very vigilant in this area.

ADDRESSING THE SPIRITUAL, PHYSICAL, AND MENTAL/EMOTIONAL:

How easily do you lose focus? Are there things you can do to regain focus in your life? What are the areas of your life that deserve your undivided focus at this time? What is the single most important area of focus for you today? In the case of the driver, his physical need for sleep greatly affected his focus. Are there things you can do physically that would enhance your focus?

Date_____

NO X-CUSES!

Journal

"The first rule of focus is this: Wherever you are, be there."
—Author Unknown

_____
_____
_____
_____
_____
_____
_____
_____
_____
_____
_____
_____
_____
_____
_____
_____
_____
_____
_____
_____
_____
_____
_____
_____
_____
_____
_____
_____
_____
_____
_____
_____

Date_____

NO X-CUSES!

Physical

Did you exercise today? ☐ yes ☐ no

What exercise did you do?

Did you eat healthy today? ☐ yes ☐ no

Did you get enough sleep? ☐ yes ☐ no

Did you drink enough water? ☐ yes ☐ no

Did you take your vitamins/supplements? ☐ yes ☐ no

Spiritual

Did you do your Bible reading today? ☐ yes ☐ no

What did you read?

Did you pray today? ☐ yes ☐ no

What did you pray about?

Mental/Emotional

What positive books/magazines did you read?

Did you spend personal thought-time today? ☐ yes ☐ no

What positive words did you speak to others?

What positive CDs did you listen to?

Day 12

THE ANSWER YOU DO NOT WANT

"Acceptance of what has happened is the first step to
overcoming the consequences of any misfortune."
—William James

Devastating events prove to be life-changing. During these events, we hope to learn even the smallest lesson that will improve our wisdom. These events are not always easy to deal with. Many of these events mark us in such a way our lives will never be the same.

The best man I have ever known was Greg Lee. Greg and I grew up together. During our adolescence, I spent as much time at his house as I did at my own. Greg was from a solid home, and it showed in his life. A certain glow overcame a room whenever Greg entered it.

November 5, 1989, changed my life. It was the day Greg and his girlfriend had a horrific automobile accident. His girlfriend survived, while the accident would eventually take Greg's life. In just twenty-four hours after the accident, I would lose one of the best influences in my life.

I returned to town late that Saturday evening. Before going home, I stopped in town to see a friend. He told me Greg had been in an automobile accident, and they had to fly him to Vanderbilt Hospital. They were not expecting him to survive.

Immediately, I made the hour and a half drive to the hospital. I knew things were bad when I saw his brother Steven. As bad as I thought the situation was, it was even worse. Greg was literally fighting for his life. I felt so helpless! One of my best friends needed my help, and I could not do anything to help him.

I went where my faith always takes me: God. Finding myself in the chapel, I prayed with as much intensity as I could muster. I left the chapel with a peaceful feeling knowing God would heal Greg. My idea of healing and God's idea of healing were totally different. I was heartbroken when Greg died. Not only had I lost a good friend, I also felt God had let me down. I felt alone.

My life has always been steeped in the Christian lifestyle; however, during that time, I did not want anything to do with God. I did not read the Bible. I did not pray. I was angry with God. After a week, I finally broke. I began to cry and ask God why He had lied to me. During that time, God revealed to me that He did not lie. I had asked for Greg to be healed. God gave me what I had asked for. Occasionally, healing comes in the form of death! God did not promise tough times would not come. He did promise He would always be there for us.

Death was not the answer I wanted, but it was the answer I received. I learned a valuable lesson through that miserable time: I do not always know what the best is. There will be times when I do not get the answer I am looking for. Maybe, I am not even asking the right questions. I am learning to stop and access the situation when things do not go my way.

Through this and many other situations, I have learned I do not have to control everything. I have often placed myself in great peril by trying to control every situation around me. My faith has taught me God is in control. Strangely enough, all I have to do is let go and let God. Because of this traumatic experience, I changed one of my rules of life: Don't transform God to my standards. Allow God to transform me.

ADDRESSING THE SPIRITUAL, PHYSICAL, AND MENTAL/EMOTIONAL:

Do you remember a time when you did not get the answer you wanted? How did you respond? Was there a different perspective to view that situation? How do you now respond when you do not get the answer you want? In what ways can you learn from these situations? How can you use these times to strengthen your faith in God?

Date_____

NO X-CUSES!

Journal

"God, grant me the serenity to accept the things I cannot
change, the courage to change the things I can, and the
wisdom to know the difference."
—Reinhold Niebuhr

_____
_____
_____
_____
_____
_____
_____
_____
_____
_____
_____
_____
_____
_____
_____
_____
_____
_____
_____
_____
_____
_____
_____
_____
_____
_____
_____
_____
_____
_____

Date_____

NO X-CUSES!

Physical

Did you exercise today? ☐ yes ☐ no

What exercise did you do?

Did you eat healthy today? ☐ yes ☐ no

Did you get enough sleep? ☐ yes ☐ no

Did you drink enough water? yes ☐ no

Did you take your vitamins/supplements? ☐ yes ☐ no

Spiritual

Did you do your Bible reading today? ☐ yes ☐ no

What did you read?

Did you pray today? ☐ yes ☐ no

What did you pray about?

Mental/Emotional

What positive books/magazines did you read?

Did you spend personal thought-time today? ☐ yes ☐ no

What positive words did you speak to others?

What positive CDs did you listen to?

ASKING FOR HELP

"I understand now that the vulnerability I've always felt is the greatest strength a person can have. You can't experience life without feeling life. What I've learned is that being vulnerable to somebody you love is not a weakness, it's a strength."
—Elisabeth Shue

Paul, the apostle, wrote about his "thorn in the flesh" (2 Corinthians 12:7, NIV). While we do not exactly know what his "thorn" was, I can empathize with him. I have my own "thorn in the flesh." While not alone, I share mine with millions of other people. My "thorn" is depression.

Most people who know me would not even start to think I have struggled with depression. I have struggled with it for over thirty years. I have had a depression problem more than half of my life. What a staggering thought! I may have depression, but depression does not have me—anymore! For me, it is a matter of attitude. Depression only has us if we engage in the mindset that it is something for which to be ashamed. It is a biochemical disorder I can control with the help of my doctors.

My struggle can be controlled with medication. There are those who disagree with this. I grew up listening to preachers say, "Just give it to Jesus." I was trying my best to do just that. Every time I tried, things just became worse. It was a downward spiral that seemed to get worse until I could not even function on a daily basis. It is my opinion; however, I believe that the church should not be in the business of diagnosing medical diseases.

Millions of people, including myself, have tried to solve this problem on their own. Impossible. While trying to handle the problem alone, my life only became more tedious. I grew up with the philosophy, "the harder you work the more success you enjoy." I was working really hard, but I was not receiving any success. I was at my "wits-end."

In order to stop the chaos in my life, I knew I had to take charge. Even though it seems like an paradox, I had to give up control in order to have it. For me, this meant I had to seek professional help. I was thinking thoughts a "normal" person should not think.

With the help of a friend, I entered myself into a psychiatric unit at a well-established hospital. Although I love the outdoors this was the only way to receive the intense therapy that I needed. I felt helpless and hopeless at the same time. Safety was what I needed to feel in order to find the help I desperately craved.

That day was a turning point for me. I found people who were willing to help me through the tough times. With the confidence of that help, I have once again taken control of my life. "Take captive every thought and make it submissive to Christ (2 Corinthians 10:5)." I still need the assistance of anti-depressant medication. Along with a great therapist, I continue to work on many issues. I found something I really needed: help. It was there all the time; I just had to ask for it.

Through this experience, I developed the "H-Cubed (H³) Principle." This Principle states:

1) We are human. Superman does not exist. We are not, nor are we ever, perfect.

2) We must be humble. Ask for help. When the words were written, "No man is an island . . .," it meant that it takes all of us working together. We need the help of others.

3) We must be honest. We can't receive help until we admit our weaknesses.

ADDRESSING THE SPIRITUAL, PHYSICAL, AND MENTAL/EMOTIONAL:

What problems are you facing in which you need help? Are you afraid to ask for it? Do you trust God to help you? If not, what causes your lack of trust? Are there people you trust to help you? What can you do to help yourself? Do you need to give up control in order to gain control? If so, then how?

Date_____

NO X-CUSES!

Journal

"All of us, at certain moments of our lives need to take advice
and to receive help from other people"
—Alexis Carrel

_____
_____
_____
_____
_____
_____
_____
_____
_____
_____
_____
_____
_____
_____
_____
_____
_____
_____
_____
_____
_____
_____
_____
_____
_____
_____

Date_____

NO X-CUSES!

Physical

Did you exercise today? ☐ yes ☐ no

What exercise did you do?

Did you eat healthy today? ☐ yes ☐ no

Did you get enough sleep? ☐ yes ☐ no

Did you drink enough water? ☐ yes ☐ no

Did you take your vitamins/supplements? ☐ yes ☐ no

Spiritual

Did you do your Bible reading today? ☐ yes ☐ no

What did you read?

Did you pray today? ☐ yes ☐ no

What did you pray about?

Mental/Emotional

What positive books/magazines did you read?

Did you spend personal thought-time today? ☐ yes ☐ no

What positive words did you speak to others?

What positive CDs did you listen to?

KEEP YOUR HEAD UP

"I can't change the direction of the wind, but I can adjust my
sails to always reach my destination"
—Jimmy Dean

As I have stated earlier, I get a certain lift from my daily running.
For me, it has become "my time." My daily schedule is flexible,
except for my running, devotional, and exercise time. If I do not do
these activities on a daily basis, then my life becomes chaotic.

I have been blessed to have run in some incredible places.
Orlando, Florida provided me with some incredible early morning
runs. In Tallinnin, Estonia, as the breeze blew in from the Baltic Sea,
I was able to enjoy the early morning runs. Although those places
were inspirational, I have always had a certain familiar peace while
running in my hometown.

I grew up in a small, Southern town. For most folks, they would
consider it a boring place to be; however, as an adult, I have come
to enjoy my brief visitation stints in the old neighborhood. Mom's
house and the neighborhood still provide a welcomed relief from
my "normal" routine. While there, I am able to enjoy running a very
familiar, serene path.

While in my hometown, I usually run the same five-mile route.
It provides some challenges: one semi-tough hill, some incline, and
some well-enjoyed flat stretches. Even though it is familiar, it still
challenges me. Some days, the running is tougher than others.

One day stands out among all the others. A utility company
provided an additional challenge to my route. The local water
department was digging up the shoulder of the roadway in order
to put in new water lines. For some, these circumstances posed no
inconvenience. For me, it provided insight into my daily life.

During the last mile of my run, I have a long straight stretch. Just past the straight stretch is a bend in the road, and just past that curve is my finish line. It was a blazing, hot summer day, and I was hot and tired. The humidity set the tone for my lack of focus. In middle Tennessee, the humidity combined with the summer heat would cause Satan to smile.

Normally when I run, I keep my head up. It is vitally important to know where I am going. But on this day, I found myself constantly looking down to make sure my footing was stable. The utility work project had caused my normal smooth running surface to have a less that desired rocky foundation. Instead of maintaining correct running form, I began to slump over in order to keep an eye on where my feet were landing.

During this process, I was not aware of my breathing pattern. Using incorrect form, I found myself out of my "zone." All of us have a "zone."—A time in which everything is clicking just right, providing us with the opportunity for maximum achievement. On this day, I was struggling. If I did not change something, then I would not be able to finish my run.

Suddenly, it dawned on me. My form was incorrect. I began to assess what was going wrong. In that quick moment, I recognized that my struggle was caused by one simple thing: I had lost sight of my destination. By forgetting to keep my head up and my eye on the target, I began looking down, causing me to slump over as I ran, thus closing down my lung capacity. My lack of attention toward my destination almost caused me to not be able to finish. I was so busy looking at the distractions I almost forgot where I was headed.

ADDRESSING THE SPIRITUAL, PHYSICAL, AND MENTAL/EMOTIONAL:

Have you forgotten your destination? Where are you eventually heading? What does your "finish line" look like? What things have you distracted? What can you do to refocus yourself on your destination? What will it take for you to keep your head up?

Date_____

NO X-CUSES!

Journal

"Obstacles are those frightful things you see when you take
your eyes off the goal."
—Henry Ford

_____
_____
_____
_____
_____
_____
_____
_____
_____
_____
_____
_____
_____
_____
_____
_____
_____
_____
_____
_____
_____
_____
_____
_____
_____
_____
_____
_____
_____
_____

Date_____

NO X-CUSES!

Physical

Did you exercise today? ☐ yes ☐ no

What exercise did you do?

Did you eat healthy today? ☐ yes ☐ no

Did you get enough sleep? ☐ yes ☐ no

Did you drink enough water? ☐ yes ☐ no

Did you take your vitamins/supplements? ☐ yes ☐ no

Spiritual

Did you do your Bible reading today? ☐ yes ☐ no

What did you read?

Did you pray today? ☐ yes ☐ no

What did you pray about?

Mental/Emotional

What positive books/magazines did you read?

Did you spend personal thought-time today? ☐ yes ☐ no

What positive words did you speak to others?

What positive CDs did you listen to?

Day 15

OUR DRIVING THOUGHTS

"As a single footstep will not make a path on earth, so a single
thought will not make a pathway in the mind. To make a deep
physical path, we walk ceaselessly again and again. To make
a deep mental path, we must think over and over the kinds of
thoughts we wish to dominate our lives."
—Henry David Thoreau

Consciously or unconsciously, we have thoughts that drive us to do what we do. These thoughts may have been with us for the better part of our lives. As we discover these thoughts, we struggle to find their foundations. All we know is they have become a major force in our lives.

As I write this, I have recently become aware of some of my driving thoughts. I have affectionally named them my "mind talk." My mind talk has been embedded with me since I was about six years old. The major theme of my mind talk started because I was sexually abused as a child. Although I strive constantly to be a positive person, I have found my thoughts can be negative and destructive.

One of my abusers (yes, there were others) once told me, "Don't tell anybody. Nobody cares! Nobody is going to help you anyway." Who says words do not have power. By the request of my therapist, I have written these words on an index card, and I keep them in my wallet. These words have echoed in my mind for over thirty years! Because of these words, I have always tried to handle life with a "lone ranger" mentality. By listening to these words, I have found myself in some lonely and miserable situations.

Until recently, these words have driven my life. Along with the by-products of the sexual abuse, I allowed these words to produce in me a sense of frustration and unworthiness. With the help of my therapist, I have learned to "take captive every thought" (2 Corinthians 10:5). Every time these thoughts present themselves, I have to take out my index card and read audibly what my abuser said to me. By doing this, I have come to realize the power I have given to these words. These words do have power only because I have given them power. This exercise has also allowed me to see how wrong these words are. I have people in my life who love me and want to help me. Am I giving them the chance to do so? In the past the answer has been "no," but now I am trying my best to give them the chance.

"Mind talk" is a major ingredient to impact our life. It affected my perception of life. After listening to my "mind talk," I often struggled with trusting myself, others and God. Thus, I allowed it to greatly affect all aspects of my life by remolding how I perceived the physical, spiritual, and mental/emotional.

<u>ADDRESSING THE SPIRITUAL, PHYSICAL, AND MENTAL/EMOTIONAL:</u>

Is there mind talk that is driving your life? What caused them? How do they live themselves out in your daily life? How can you "take every thought captive?" What activity can you do to reverse the power of these thoughts and words? What words do you give power in your life?

Date_____

NO X-CUSES!

Journal

"In the province of the mind, what one believes to be true
either is true or becomes true."
—John Lilly

_____
_____
_____
_____
_____
_____
_____
_____
_____
_____
_____
_____
_____
_____
_____
_____
_____
_____
_____
_____
_____
_____
_____
_____
_____
_____
_____
_____
_____

Date_____

NO X-CUSES!

Physical

Did you exercise today? ☐ yes ☐ no

What exercise did you do?

Did you eat healthy today? ☐ yes ☐ no

Did you get enough sleep? ☐ yes ☐ no

Did you drink enough water? yes ☐ no

Did you take your vitamins/supplements? ☐ yes ☐ no

Spiritual

Did you do your Bible reading today? ☐ yes ☐ no

What did you read?

Did you pray today? ☐ yes ☐ no

What did you pray about?

Mental/Emotional

What positive books/magazines did you read?

Did you spend personal thought-time today? ☐ yes ☐ no

What positive words did you speak to others?

What positive CDs did you listen to?

PERSONAL INTEGRITY

"Have the courage to say no. Have the courage to face the
truth. Do the right thing because it is right. These are the
magic keys to living your life with integrity."
—W. Clement Stone

I have always considered myself a man of integrity. Two years
ago, I attended a conference, which changed my mind. Now I realize,
for me to have integrity, I have to keep my appointments. If I say I
am going to do something, then I must always follow through on it.

I remember that conference well. The leader said, "A broken
promise is a cry for help." She evidently knew me well, because I
was a man who continually broke my promises, and in my own way,
I was crying out for help. During that conference, I was afforded the
opportunity to see how my life was full of broken promises. I was
guilty of not living up to my word.

One area of my life that really provides a challenge for me is my
schedule. I have a tendency to overbook. People-pleasing has always
been one of my biggest hang-ups. By trying to please everyone, I
stretch myself too thin, thus accomplishing very little.

I began to understand one thing: trying to please everybody
stemmed from my self-centeredness. Deep down, I felt this need
to be important. In order to be this, I needed people to depend on
me. Being needed by others, I constantly fed my ego. What a sad
statement about my life. By now understanding who I am, I no
longer feel the need to create this false sense of security.

My whole lifestyle of over commitment and people-pleasing
had really stripped away my integrity. I promised to meet people
at certain times, and I would be a half hour late. This told two
valuable things about me. The first thing was I thought my time

was more important than other people's time, and the second was that my promises did not mean much. In essence, I had become the self-centered liar I never wanted to be.

How has that realization changed my life? Now, I always try to be on time. If I find myself running late, then I call the other person and let them know. Do I always do this? No, but I am more cognizant of other people's time and feelings.

ADDRESSING THE SPIRITUAL, PHYSICAL, AND MENTAL/EMOTIONAL:

Do you over commit? Why? Do you promise things and not deliver? What are they? Are you consistently running late for your appointments? What can you do to make sure you value other people's time? How are you self-centered? Time is a non-renewable resource. Not only am I to value and respect my time, I am also to value and respect other people's time as well.

Special note to pastors:

After serving as a professional clergy for over twelve years, I have found clergy to be especially guilty of being late for appointments. There is an underlying belief that people will understand because of your position. As leaders of your congregation, you set the example! I urge you to be sensitive to other people's time. You must live up to your word. You must be people of integrity.

Date_____

NO X-CUSES!

Journal

"I could never think well of a man's intellectual or moral
character, if he was habitually unfaithful to his appointments."
—Nathaniel Emmons

Date_____

NO X-CUSES!

__Physical__

Did you exercise today? ☐ yes ☐ no

What exercise did you do?

Did you eat healthy today? ☐ yes ☐ no

Did you get enough sleep? ☐ yes ☐ no

Did you drink enough water? ☐ yes ☐ no

Did you take your vitamins/supplements? ☐ yes ☐ no

__Spiritual__

Did you do your Bible reading today? ☐ yes ☐ no

What did you read?

Did you pray today? ☐ yes ☐ no

What did you pray about?

Mental/Emotional

What positive books/magazines did you read?

Did you spend personal thought-time today? ☐ yes ☐ no

What positive words did you speak to others?

What positive CDs did you listen to?

ADAPTIVITY

"The human brain is still undergoing rapid adaptive evolution."
—Howard Hughes

Few people in our modern-day world really live up to the term "hero." I have been blessed and honored to know one who does. His name is Dave Stevens. Regardless of his numerous accolades in life, who he really is classifies him as a hero. Real heroes are heroes all their lives.

Dave is a highly decorated, retired Navy F-15 pilot. To be a commander of such a powerful aircraft requires one to honor him with respect. He worked long and hard to reach that level during his military career. His growth and learning did not stop there. Since his retirement from the Navy, he has continued the growing process.

I have known Dave over thirteen years. For the dominant period of that time, he has demonstrated the tendency to be quiet and introverted. Although the old adage says people do not change, I am a witness of the invalidity of that statement, especially in regards to Dave Stevens. Over the period of these years, I have watched him change into an extroverted, people-person, who is compassionate about helping others change their lives. The metamorphosis has been mesmerizing.

How did Dave accomplish such a feat? He drew upon wise counsel. He trusted others who had already accomplished this feat. He enlisted strong mentors and then followed their examples. Even though I consider Dave a hero for his service to our country, he embodies the term "hero" for being strong enough to change. Today, Dave is a leader in his professional field. He speaks to thousands of people about the power of goals and change. The world needs more Dave Stevens in it!

Dave realized some valuable things that helped him change:

1) We are never too old to learn. When we quit learning, we start dying.

2) Be very careful who you choose to be your mentor. "Not everyone has the right to speak into your life."—Charles Mason

3) Listen intently, learn, and then put into practice.

ADDRESSING THE SPIRITUAL, PHYSICAL, AND MENTAL/EMOTIONAL:

How can you be more adaptable? Do you believe you can change? Are you willing to trust the advice of a mentor? In your spiritual life, can you trust God? Is your God able to change you? How can we listen better to the positive influences around us?

Date_____

NO X-CUSES!

Journal

"If we don't change, we don't grow. If we don't grow, we
aren't really living."
—Gail Sheehy

Date_____

NO X-CUSES!

<u>Physical</u>

Did you exercise today? ☐ yes ☐ no

What exercise did you do?

Did you eat healthy today? ☐ yes ☐ no

Did you get enough sleep? ☐ yes ☐ no

Did you drink enough water? ☐ yes ☐ no

Did you take your vitamins/supplements? ☐ yes ☐ no

<u>Spiritual</u>

Did you do your Bible reading today? ☐ yes ☐ no

What did you read?

Did you pray today? ☐ yes ☐ no

What did you pray about?

Mental/Emotional

What positive books/magazines did you read?

Did you spend personal thought-time today? ☐ yes ☐ no

What positive words did you speak to others?

What positive CDs did you listen to?

LISTEN TO YOUR GUT

"I live on my gut instinct."
—Melanie Brown

Bryan Hill is the man who literally altered my life. Although it did not happen in a "superhero" kind of way, I still give him the credit. Even though he is only two years older than I, his maturity taught him to live a non-assuming, humble life. To this day, Bryan does not know what he did for me.

The setting for the event was established because of a very troubled childhood event of mine. The scenario had caused me great difficulty of which I was not handling well. As you read this, keep in mind, I was only fourteen. Even when everything is perfect, most fourteen-year olds do not think rationally. Tragedy is the by-product when trauma is added to the mix.

One particular night, I felt I had experienced enough pain. I loaded a gun, cocked the hammer, and was ready to pull the trigger. As fate would have it, the phone rang. For some reason, I answered the phone call which changed my life's destiny.

Bryan was prompted to call and check on me. He was involved in his spiritual devotions when he had an insatiable urge to call me. He called and said, "I just called to say I love you. Bye!" I was within an inch of ending my life. How was I supposed to respond to such a phone call?

Needless to say, the phone call came at the most opportune moment. What would have happened had Bryan not followed his "gut instinct?" By following his intuition, he reminded me of an important fact: I had people who loved and cared about me.

Following your gut requires:

1) Listening to the universe. This requires one to be able to be quiet.

2) DO! Respond when prompted to do something—Be Bold.

3) Be Vulnerable.

ADDRESSING THE SPIRITUAL, PHYSICAL, AND MENTAL/EMOTIONAL:

Are you being urged to do something positive? Is there something you need to do for someone? Is there something you need to say to someone? How will this impact your life spiritually, mentally/emotionally, or physically? More importantly, how will this affect someone else's life? With your words, you have the power to change someone else's life! How will you use that power and opportunity?

Date_____

NO X-CUSES!

Journal

"There is a vitality, a life force, an energy, a quickening, that is translated through you into action, and because there is only one of you in all time, this expression is unique. And if you block it, it will never exist through any other medium and will be lost."
—Martha Graham

_____
_____
_____
_____
_____
_____
_____
_____
_____
_____
_____
_____
_____
_____
_____
_____
_____
_____
_____
_____
_____
_____
_____
_____
_____
_____

Mark Beecham

Date_____

NO X-CUSES!

Physical

Did you exercise today? ☐ yes ☐ no

What exercise did you do?

Did you eat healthy today? ☐ yes ☐ no

Did you get enough sleep? ☐ yes ☐ no

Did you drink enough water? ☐ yes ☐ no

Did you take your vitamins/supplements? ☐ yes ☐ no

Spiritual

Did you do your Bible reading today? ☐ yes ☐ no

What did you read?

Did you pray today? ☐ yes ☐ no

What did you pray about?

Mental/Emotional

What positive books/magazines did you read?

Did you spend personal thought-time today? ☐ yes ☐ no

What positive words did you speak to others?

What positive CDs did you listen to?

Day 19

YOU GIVE YOU GET

"Don't live down to expectations. Go out there and do
something remarkable."
—Wendy Wasserstein

Even though my grade point average does not warrant it, I have been labeled as being a scholar. During my sophomore year of college, I was selected to be a recipient of the Zimmerman Jewish Scholars program. Because of this honor, I was able to attend the summer session at Hebrew University in Jerusalem, Israel. The experience afforded me the opportunity to learn a great lesson: Regardless of language or nationality, people are basically the same. We all want to be loved and respected.

On the return flight from that experience, I was on the receiving end of my new found knowledge. Murphy's law ("Whatever can go wrong, will go wrong.") was in effect. The morning of our departure flight, the Israeli airport personnel went on strike. That strike caused me a personal crisis. My return to the United States (home of fried potatoes and cornbread) depended on that airplane!

After some turns of good luck, I was able to fly out of the Tel Aviv Airport that evening. My original flight plans had to be rescheduled. Instead of flying to New York and then to Nashville, I had to take the long way back home. My new plans called for me to fly to Paris, France, lay over ten hours, and then fly to Newark, New Jersey. After laying over in Newark, I would then get to fly to Nashville. The journey proved to be a long day.

By the time I reached Newark, I was completely exhausted. My friends and I were tired and irritable. Nothing against New Jersey, I just wanted to be home in Tennessee. I had not slept in my own bed for several weeks, and I wanted to go home. At that point, we met the nicest employee Continental Airlines had to offer.

Although I do not remember her name now, her smile is forever etched in my mind. After explaining our dilemma, she wanted to get "these Southern gentlemen home as quickly as she could." Even though she tried to get us on an earlier flight, we were stuck in the airport for another five hours until our flight departed. It was her friendly, thoughtful attitude that stuck with me.

At the time, I paused to write down her name. After arriving home, the next business day, I called Continental Airlines to report what a great job the employee had done. The customer service agent on the phone was surprised. "We never get any positive comments on that terminal! People only call to complain." was her response. The statement shocked me. I only found nice, positive people in that terminal. Could it be because those were the kind of people for which I was looking?

That lady could have easily just done her job; however, she was enthusiastic to help us. She made an impression on me. To this day, whenever I think of New Jersey, I always smile. She gave to us and in turn she received.

Even though I did not know it at the time, I was living out my newfound knowledge. By calling the airlines and commenting on her job performance, she received a positive job performance award. I did not know it, but I was giving back to her what she had given to us. Thankfully, it did not end there. Because of taking the time to call in and report her good job performance, Continental Airlines sent me a box of Christie Cookies. After all that, I received another gift. What a great country!!

ADDRESSING THE SPIRITUAL, PHYSICAL, AND MENTAL/EMOTIONAL:

How can you give kindness to others? Are there specific people to which you need to return an act of kindness? On a daily basis, what opportunities arise for you to share kindness and compassion with others? Can you repay someone else's kindness by sharing it with another person? How can you be more "tuned in" to the positive attitudes around you?

Date_____

NO X-CUSES!

Journal

"You can get anything you want in life, as long as you help enough other people get what they want without expecting anything in return."
—Zig Ziglar

Date_____

NO X-CUSES!

Physical

Did you exercise today? ☐ yes ☐ no

What exercise did you do?

Did you eat healthy today? ☐ yes ☐ no

Did you get enough sleep? ☐ yes ☐ no

Did you drink enough water? ☐ yes ☐ no

Did you take your vitamins/supplements? ☐ yes ☐ no

Spiritual

Did you do your Bible reading today? ☐ yes ☐ no

What did you read?

Did you pray today? ☐ yes ☐ no

What did you pray about?

Mental/Emotional

What positive books/magazines did you read?

Did you spend personal thought-time today? ☐ yes ☐ no

What positive words did you speak to others?

What positive CDs did you listen to?

GETTING BACK UP

"Wherever you go, go with all your heart."
—Confucius

Every person has someone special in his or her life. This particular special friend is of the four-legged variety. Smokey is a full-blooded, grand champion blue tick coon hound. Being a huge University of Tennessee Volunteer fan, I named Smokey after the mascot of the university. Smokey is my special friend, and he is also my pet dog (just do not tell him he is a dog).

Recently, Smokey underwent an incredible ordeal in his life. While on an excursion at my mom's house, Smokey contracted parvo, a debilitating disease that wreaks havoc on a dog's intestines. I have had other blue tick hounds die of this disease. It is heartbreaking to watch and know there is nothing that can be done. The outlook was bleak. Our family veterinarian said Smokey had a 50/50 chance of surviving. Somebody forgot to tell him about the bleak odds of his survival.

Our vet continued to deliberate about how bleak Smokey's chances of survival were. I constantly debated him on that fact. I knew my dog would get better. After much suffering, Smokey won. After three and a half weeks, the vet released him to come home. The healing process was on-going and took several months to complete. Every day, Smokey made improvements. The vet even commented about the strong-willed nature of Smokey.

In life, we will all experience tough times. We will be bruised, broken, and sometimes, bloodied. Pain is part of life. As my friend Aaron Potts says, "It is not how you get knocked down that counts. It is how high you bounce back up!" Smokey bounced back from this experience and became a stronger dog for it.

This experience taught me one very valuable lesson in life. It is included in my list of rules for living: "It's not the size of the dog in the fight that counts. It is the size of the fight in the dog that makes the difference!" The one thing about tenacity that should be well noted. The ones who get back on their feet are always twice as strong as those who have never been knocked down.

ADDRESSING THE SPIRITUAL, PHYSICAL, AND MENTAL/EMOTIONAL:

In what ways have you been knocked down or run over? How can you get up stronger? How can you use your pain to grow into a stronger person? What have these pains taught you on an emotional and spiritual level?

Date_____

NO X-CUSES!

Journal

"No matter how far life pushes you down, no matter how much you hurt, you can always bounce back."
—Sheryl Swoops

_____
_____
_____
_____
_____
_____
_____
_____
_____
_____
_____
_____
_____
_____
_____
_____
_____
_____
_____
_____
_____
_____
_____
_____
_____
_____
_____

Date_____

NO X-CUSES!

Physical

Did you exercise today? ☐ yes ☐ no

What exercise did you do?

Did you eat healthy today? ☐ yes ☐ no

Did you get enough sleep? ☐ yes ☐ no

Did you drink enough water? ☐ yes ☐ no

Did you take your vitamins/supplements? ☐ yes ☐ no

Spiritual

Did you do your Bible reading today? ☐ yes ☐ no

What did you read?

Did you pray today? ☐ yes ☐ no

What did you pray about?

Mental/Emotional

What positive books/magazines did you read?

Did you spend personal thought-time today? ☐ yes ☐ no

What positive words did you speak to others?

What positive CDs did you listen to?

OUR INFLUENCE

"You can never really live anyone else's life, not even your
child's. The influence you exert is through your own life, and
what you've become yourself."
—Eleanor Roosevelt

One of my heroes was Reverend Johnny Adams. "Brother
Johnny," as he was affectionally known, was a positive influence
on his hometown for 80+ years. His loyalty is second to none.
Growing up, he was my pastor, even though I did not attend church
regularly. He would often visit our home just to see how my family
was making it. The impressive thing is that he visited many people
every afternoon and evening after he had already worked a full day
at his vigorously, exhausting job. To me, that spells devotion.

After his "retirement," he would sit in the front pew at church.
Often times, the pastor would ask Brother Johnny to lead the
congregation in prayer. I can still hear his words: "Dear beloved,
sweet, Heavenly Father, we love you today with all our hearts." That
prayer has been forever etched on my heart.

The fantastic thing about Brother Johnny was his sensitive heart.
As he would pray, he would often be overcome with emotion. To this
day, as I sit in church, I can still visualize Brother Johnny leading
the congregation in prayer. His sensitivity was contagious. The real
reason he was so sensitive was because of his spiritual relationship
with God. When he would pray to God, he would realize he was
really praying to his best friend.

The years before his death were tough on Brother Johnny. After
being married for over fifty years, his wife died. After all those years,
their love still burned for each other. If I could only find a lady like
Mrs. Edith, then I would get married today. Even before his death,
he would dream about his bride. Something tells me that Brother

Johnny could have taught an incredible workshop on building a marriage based upon spiritual principles.

At age 90, Brother Johnny would still walk every day. He was not as fast as he once was. Before his death, he would use a walker for assistance. When I hear people's excuses for not exercising, I think about Brother Johnny Adams. It would do well for us to follow his example.

The only way to judge a man or woman's life is by looking at the people he or she has touched. As I think about Brother Johnny Adams, I think about literally hundreds whose lives have been changed. I am thankful to have had Johnny Adam's influence in my life. For that fact, hundreds of other people can say the same thing.

I have often asked myself, "What made Johnny Adam's life so effective?" I believe it to have been his strong spiritual connection. He realized the important things in life are unseen. His sense of faith unconsciously drove him to make the world a better place simply by his presence. Could we be so lucky as to be the same way?

Johnny Adams taught me three important lessons about life:

1) People, not stuff, are the important things.

2) Take time to listen. You care most with your ears.

3) Love and then there is not time to pass judgment.

ADDRESSING THE SPIRITUAL, PHYSICAL, AND MENTAL/EMOTIONAL:

How can we get in touch with our spiritual self? Do you know people like Johnny Adams? What sets them apart? What characteristic would you like to take apply to your own life?

Date_____

NO X-CUSES!

Journal

"You don't have to be a "person of influence" to be
influential. In fact, the most influential people in my life are
probably not even aware of the things they've taught me."
—Scott Adams

_____
_____
_____
_____
_____
_____
_____
_____
_____
_____
_____
_____
_____
_____
_____
_____
_____
_____
_____
_____
_____
_____
_____
_____
_____
_____
_____
_____
_____

Date_____

NO X-CUSES!

Physical

Did you exercise today? ☐ yes ☐ no

What exercise did you do?

Did you eat healthy today? ☐ yes ☐ no

Did you get enough sleep? ☐ yes ☐ no

Did you drink enough water? yes ☐ no

Did you take your vitamins/supplements? ☐ yes ☐ no

Spiritual

Did you do your Bible reading today? ☐ yes ☐ no

What did you read?

Did you pray today? ☐ yes ☐ no

What did you pray about?

Mental/Emotional

What positive books/magazines did you read?

Did you spend personal thought-time today? ☐ yes ☐ no

What positive words did you speak to others?

What positive CDs did you listen to?

HALF-WAY POINT

The half-way point is a prime opportunity to do an assessment. There is a difference between a judgment and an assessment. Assessments are evaluations to make one stronger. How has your life changed? Which goals have you accomplished? How can you better focus on the daily completion of these tasks?

Are you making progress in the three areas of focus? How has your spiritual life changed? In what ways can you more clearly focus spiritually? How has your life changed physically? Are you healthier? Are you exercising and eating healthy? If not, how can you be more clearly focused? How is your mental/emotional life? Is your thinking positive and productive? Are you expanding your knowledge? How can you improve your mental/emotional life?

"Being confident of this, that he who began a good work
in you will carry it on to completion until the day of Christ
Jesus."
—Philippians 1:6, NIV

PAYING IT FORWARD

"Easing the load for others is the greatest calling to live."
—Robbie Raines

Several years ago, there was a movie entitled, *Pay It Forward*. Although it is not my intent to unveil the plot of the movie, its central theme is doing good deeds for others. In a society that is concentrated on self-serving interests, the movie was very thought-provoking. The movie caused me to concentrate on people who are definitely passing their good fortunes on to others.

One person who has been instrumental in passing on good fortune is a lady most people call "Miss Robbie." However, I am blessed and privileged to call her "Granny." It is so wonderful just to think about how our lives crossed. Our paths crossed as a result of one of my pastoral appointments. Granny had been a member of that church for years. Our friendship started with a little booklet called <u>Grace</u>. Often times in my prayers and sermons, I speak fervently about God's grace. I contend people are beaten up enough at work and home for six days a week. As we gather for worship, we should build up and not tear down.

After hearing several of those prayers and sermons, Granny stopped by the church to deliver to me a copy of the booklet. I still have that booklet, and I will have it until I die. I lived down the street from her. That arrangement afforded me the pleasure to really get to know her. What a blessing it has been!

Granny grew up poor. She definitely knows the value of a dollar. She also knows the importance of an education. One of her dreams in life has been to establish an educational foundation to help young people obtain a college degree. I have been blessed to watch this dream become a reality for her. Currently, the Clark & Robbie Raines Scholarship Foundation gives annual scholarships to deserving students. Her life has been filled with good deeds for others.

Granny also gives to others anonymously. Within the past few years, she received a local award for the good deeds she has accomplished in our community. The ironic part is that they only listed a small fraction of the things she has accomplished. God is the only one who really knows all the good deeds she has done. She has made the world a better place. I have often asked myself, "How can I make a difference in the world?" I look at people like Robbie Raines, and I am inspired to pay it forward.

Granny has lived by three principles that she often quoted to me:

1) Do good.

2) Do good quietly.

3) Helping others is the only thing that lives on after we are gone.

ADDRESSING THE SPIRITUAL, PHYSICAL, AND MENTAL/EMOTIONAL:

What are some things we can do to lighten the burden of others? How much time can we give up in order to help others? What financial amount can we invest into the lives of others? How can our spiritual lives be inspired to help others? How have others blessed us? What spiritual responsibility do we have to bless others?

Date_____

NO X-CUSES!

Journal

"How wonderful it is that nobody need wait a single moment
before starting to improve the world."
—Anne Frank

_____
_____
_____
_____
_____
_____
_____
_____
_____
_____
_____
_____
_____
_____
_____
_____
_____
_____
_____
_____
_____
_____
_____
_____
_____
_____
_____
_____
_____

Date_____

NO X-CUSES!

Physical

Did you exercise today? ☐ yes ☐ no

What exercise did you do?

Did you eat healthy today? ☐ yes ☐ no

Did you get enough sleep? ☐ yes ☐ no

Did you drink enough water? yes ☐ no

Did you take your vitamins/supplements? ☐ yes ☐ no

Spiritual

Did you do your Bible reading today? ☐ yes ☐ no

What did you read?

Did you pray today? ☐ yes ☐ no

What did you pray about?

Mental/Emotional

What positive books/magazines did you read?

Did you spend personal thought-time today? ☐ yes ☐ no

What positive words did you speak to others?

What positive CDs did you listen to?

CHARACTER

"Character is like a tree and reputation like a shadow. The
shadow is what we think of it; the tree is the real thing."
—Abraham Lincoln

J. C. Watts, former University of Oklahoma quarterback and U.S.
Congressman said, "Character is doing what's right when nobody
is looking." What an incredible definition! Character seems to be
lacking in our society, with the exception being that of my friend
Lanny Blackwood.

Lanny has devoted his life to being a role model for young
kids. He is a husband, teacher, and coach. Although Lanny exudes
personality, his greatest trait is his character. With Lanny, what you
see is what you get, and what you get is a class act.

A few years ago, Lanny caught a fellow coach playing an ineligible
player. Instead of exposing the ineligible player, Lanny talked to
the coach. Lanny opted to give the other coach the opportunity to
"step up to the plate" and take responsibility for his actions. The
coach opted for the easy way. He kept his cheating quiet. Lanny was
terribly disappointed in the coach.

What did Lanny do? He did exactly what he has always done.
Day in and day out, he was and is a positive, honest, and productive
teacher and human being. He could have chosen to cut corners and
cheat, too, in order to "level the playing field." Lanny cannot do
those types of things. His character will not allow it.

Lanny Blackwood taught me about character, and he does so
quietly. He taught me that people with character:

1) Focus on their own actions. "I am responsible to be the best
   me I can be."

Mark Beecham

2) Realize "Winners never cheat, and cheaters never win." Eventually, the only one you cheat is yourself.

3) Life is tougher when you choose to live with character. There is no easy way out.

ADDRESSING THE SPIRITUAL, PHYSICAL, AND MENTAL/EMOTIONAL:

Are you taking the easy way out? Are you living in such a way as to be a person of character? Are you living as a person of character in your physical life, your mental/emotional life, and your spiritual life? How do you really act when no one else is watching?

Date_____

NO X-CUSES!

Journal

"Personality can open doors, but only character can keep them open."
—Elmer G. Letterman

_____
_____
_____
_____
_____
_____
_____
_____
_____
_____
_____
_____
_____
_____
_____
_____
_____
_____
_____
_____
_____
_____
_____
_____
_____
_____
_____
_____
_____

Date_____

NO X-CUSES!

Physical

Did you exercise today? ☐ yes ☐ no

What exercise did you do?

Did you eat healthy today? ☐ yes ☐ no

Did you get enough sleep? ☐ yes ☐ no

Did you drink enough water? ☐ yes ☐ no

Did you take your vitamins/supplements? ☐ yes ☐ no

Spiritual

Did you do your Bible reading today? ☐ yes ☐ no

What did you read?

Did you pray today? ☐ yes ☐ no

What did you pray about?

Mental/Emotional

What positive books/magazines did you read?

Did you spend personal thought-time today? ☐ yes ☐ no

What positive words did you speak to others?

What positive CDs did you listen to?

Day 24

WE FIND WHAT WE LOOK FOR

"Be the change you want to see in the world."
—Ghandi

A valued friend of mine, Bob Haynes, told me a story I will never forget: The story revolved around a man entering a town for the first time. He was contemplating moving into the town, so he stopped at a gas station to get some counsel. He asked the attendant, "What kind of people live here?" The attendant replied with his own question, "What kind of people live in the town from where you are moving?" the man replied, "They were mean, nosey, arrogant, pushy, and obnoxious!" to which the attendant replied, "The same kind of folks live here, too."

The gas station attendant was a wise man. He realized we always find what we are looking for. A minister taught me this story very well. He was leaving the church, and I was coming on staff. His attitude was much like the man in the story.

The minister wanted to have lunch with me and "give me some information about the church." I had lunch with the man, and he warned me that the church was "full of pretentious, arrogant, and self-centered people." Which church did he pastor? I was a pastor at that church for several years and never observed those characteristics.

The church I pastored was loving, compassionate, and giving. I am not saying that the other characteristics did not exist. However, the positive far outweighed the negative. How could one find the same group of people to be totally different? I believe the answer is found in the story Bob told me. We really do find that for which we are looking.

My dad, who was a very wise truck driver, used to tell me, "Mark, you can find good in anybody if you just look hard enough." Now, in retrospect, I finally understand what he meant.

We must be that for which we are looking. In order to find nice people, we must be nice. In order to find loving people, we must be loving. In order to find peaceful people, then we better be peaceful. This is not rocket science! The universe returns to us that which we give. Some call it karma, but I call it the natural order.

ADDRESSING THE SPIRITUAL, PHYSICAL, AND MENTAL/EMOTIONAL:

What are you looking for? Do you need to change your attitude so you can find better things? In what ways can you look for positive things in others? When thinking about others, do we remember they have been created in the image of God? How can that help the way we see others?

Date_____

NO X-CUSES!

Journal

There's a good spot tucked away somewhere in everybody.
You'll be a long time finding it, sometimes."
—Mark Twain

_____
_____
_____
_____
_____
_____
_____
_____
_____
_____
_____
_____
_____
_____
_____
_____
_____
_____
_____
_____
_____
_____
_____
_____
_____
_____
_____
_____
_____
_____

Date_____

NO X-CUSES!

Physical

Did you exercise today? ☐ yes ☐ no

What exercise did you do?

Did you eat healthy today? ☐ yes ☐ no

Did you get enough sleep? ☐ yes ☐ no

Did you drink enough water? ☐ yes ☐ no

Did you take your vitamins/supplements? ☐ yes ☐ no

Spiritual

Did you do your Bible reading today? ☐ yes ☐ no

What did you read?

Did you pray today? ☐ yes ☐ no

What did you pray about?

Mental/Emotional

What positive books/magazines did you read?

Did you spend personal thought-time today? ☐ yes ☐ no

What positive words did you speak to others?

What positive CDs did you listen to?

LIVING IN PEACE

"Diversity: The art of thinking independently together."
—Malcolm Forbes

I met him my freshman year of college. He was and continues to be the wisest man I have ever met. His name is Dr. Toby Williams. Although he is a man inundated with academic accolades, his wisdom and intelligence could never be measured using a textbook.

Although Dr. Williams was my Western Civilization professor, I learned much more from him than just that subject. I feel his expertise was in interpersonal relationships. He valued the person, as a person, even if they did not share his views. Respect was something that he not only demanded; it was something he extended to everybody. From him I learned this motto: "We agree, to disagree, agreeably, on seemingly non-negotiable matters."

Using Dr. Williams' motto, the world could be a peaceful place. In a time when the world seems to be crying out for peace, we could desperately put this motto into practice. Using his sense of humor and gentle spirit, Dr. Williams taught me a key component of wisdom. People do not have to agree with me for us to be able to live together in peace. After all, God does not ask us to change people. God only asks us to love people. What a profound thought!! This lesson can best be summed up in the movie, *A River Runs Through It*. The minister, when speaking about his son, said, "We can love completely without completely understanding."

Much of the conflict today exists because of our own expectations. We expect, even demand, other people to be like we are. If the rest of the world were like me, then it would be a boring place. Diversity only strengthens us. I believe real weakness is expressed by the inability to accept differences.

To live in peace with our fellow human beings, it is really simple:

1) Treat others the same way you want to be treated. The "golden rule" never tarnishes.

2) Do #1 because it is the right thing to do. What you give out will come back to you, so you better give out the best.

3) Realize diversity as an opportunity, not to sellout your moral values and individuality, but to learn from a different teacher that God has placed in your life.

> "You are still my brother and sister regardless of color, shape, size, political views, sexual orientation, or socioeconomic status. I don't have to understand everything about you. I just have to love you!"—Mark Beecham

ADDRESSING THE SPIRITUAL, PHYSICAL, AND MENTAL/EMOTIONAL:

Do I demand people to be like me? How do I treat people who are different than I am? Do I show respect to people who are different? In what ways do I forsake peace in order to be right? How do I try to change people to believe the way I believe? What can I do to live in peace with others?

Date_____

NO X-CUSES!

Journal

"Blessed are the peacemakers, for they will be called sons of
God."
—Matthew 5:9

_____
_____
_____
_____
_____
_____
_____
_____
_____
_____
_____
_____
_____
_____
_____
_____
_____
_____
_____
_____
_____
_____
_____
_____
_____
_____
_____
_____
_____
_____
_____

Date_____

NO X-CUSES!

Physical

Did you exercise today? ☐ yes ☐ no

What exercise did you do?

Did you eat healthy today? ☐ yes ☐ no

Did you get enough sleep? ☐ yes ☐ no

Did you drink enough water? ☐ yes ☐ no

Did you take your vitamins/supplements? ☐ yes ☐ no

Spiritual

Did you do your Bible reading today? ☐ yes ☐ no

What did you read?

Did you pray today? ☐ yes ☐ no

What did you pray about?

Mental/Emotional

What positive books/magazines did you read?

Did you spend personal thought-time today? ☐ yes ☐ no

What positive words did you speak to others?

What positive CDs did you listen to?

Day 26

THE VICIOUS CYCLE

"Think twice before you speak, because your words and
influence will plant the seed of either success or failure in the
mind of another."
—Napoleon Hill

Whether we like it or not, our lives are a by-product of our thoughts. We attract what we think. If our thinking is negative, our life is negative. Likewise, if our thoughts are positive, our lives are positive. If your life is not what you like, then change your thoughts. Dr. Norman Vincent Peale said it best, "Change your thoughts, and you change your world."

This begins the vicious cycle. Our actions stem from our thoughts. Our thoughts are produced from what influences we are placing in our minds. Our minds are a direct result of our actions. So, how do we stop the cycle?

In order to stop the effects of this cycle, we must be willing to be aware of our influences. First and foremost, what are you placing in your mind? Do you watch negative television shows? Do you listen to negative music? The computer term GIGO (garbage in-garbage out) describes it fully. We cannot expect to have positive thoughts if we are constantly seeing and hearing negative influences.

We change our thoughts by taking in positive influences. Les Brown, the master-motivator, says that eighty-seven percent of our self-talk is negative. If we begin with positive influences, then we change that significantly. We think between forty and fifty thousand thoughts per day. The negativity can reproduce at a rapid pace. Conversely, the positive can reproduce rapidly as well.

All of these influences and thoughts are producing for us actions. If we are experiencing negative actions, then we know we must be putting in negative influences. The strange thing is negativity breeds negativity just as positive breeds positive. If our actions are positive, then we think positive thoughts, and then we attract positive influences to us-thus starting the cycle again.

How do we break the cycle? We must be pro-active! Begin by listing the influences of your life. Then, ask yourself, "Is this influence positive or is it negative?" If it is negative, what can you do to change it? Just do it!

ADDRESSING THE SPIRITUAL, PHYSICAL, AND MENTAL/EMOTIONAL:

What positive influences can I add to my life? What negative influences do I need to take out of my life? Are there positive or motivational CD's I can listen to? Can I be more selective about the television programs I watch? Do I watch violent movies? By changing this cycle, how will it affect my life? How will this change my spiritual life? My physical life? My mental/emotional life?

Date_____

NO X-CUSES!

Journal

"Everything that has happened to you has come about because
you first saw it happening in your mind's eye."
—Galileo

_____
_____
_____
_____
_____
_____
_____
_____
_____
_____
_____
_____
_____
_____
_____
_____
_____
_____
_____
_____
_____
_____
_____
_____
_____
_____
_____
_____
_____

Date_____

NO X-CUSES!

Physical

Did you exercise today? ☐ yes ☐ no

What exercise did you do?

Did you eat healthy today? ☐ yes ☐ no

Did you get enough sleep? ☐ yes ☐ no

Did you drink enough water? ☐ yes ☐ no

Did you take your vitamins/supplements? ☐ yes ☐ no

Spiritual

Did you do your Bible reading today? ☐ yes ☐ no

What did you read?

Did you pray today? ☐ yes ☐ no

What did you pray about?

Mental/Emotional

What positive books/magazines did you read?

Did you spend personal thought-time today? ☐ yes ☐ no

What positive words did you speak to others?

What positive CDs did you listen to?

VISUALIZATION

"Throughout all history, the great wise men and teachers, philosophers, and prophets have disagreed with one another on many different things. It is only on this one point that they are in complete and unanimous agreement: We become what we think about."
—Earl Nightingale

I am quickly becoming a fitness junkie. I love the gym. For me, I find great satisfaction with the feel of a great workout. As much as I love the gym, I sometimes need extra motivation. It is because of this needed extra motivation that I discovered the power of visualization.

Visualization is an empowering reminder of what life WILL be when you accomplish your goal. I need the constant reminder of how things will be when I accomplish my goals. Since sound physical conditioning is an essential goal for me, I need to be reminded and refocused onto what I am trying to achieve. My visualization is stimulated by the many pictures I have in my home and office.

My office is bombarded with pictures of how I want my life to be. I keep a picture of my new automobile (not yet purchased) in my truck. These are constant reminders to me. I even have pictures posted on the front of my bathroom door. Why? If the mind can see it, then it can be achieved.

Does it work? Yes. From time to time, I need motivation. During these times, I mentally draw strength. If I want to end a workout early, then I think about what I want to physically look like. The mental imagery of those pictures pushes me on to do my complete workout.

As a teenager, I played baseball. One of my coaches explained to us the benefit of seeing the game played before it happened. He would often make us close our eyes and play the game in our heads. He would ask us to think about what we would do in certain situations. Did it work? Yes. After visualizing, our team became better equipped to handle those situations. As a result, we became better ballplayers.

ADDRESSING THE SPIRITUAL, PHYSICAL, AND MENTAL/EMOTIONAL:

What do you want to accomplish in life? Do you see yourself doing it? What visual reminders can you have to bring this about? What visualizations can you use to be successful in your physical life? Your spiritual life? Your mental/emotional life?

Date_____

NO X-CUSES!

Journal

"You must see your goals clearly and specifically before you can set out for them. Hold them in your mind until they become second nature."
—Les Brown

_____

_____
_____
_____
_____
_____
_____
_____
_____
_____
_____
_____
_____
_____
_____
_____
_____
_____
_____
_____
_____
_____
_____
_____
_____
_____
_____

Date_____

NO X-CUSES!

Physical

Did you exercise today? ☐ yes ☐ no

What exercise did you do?

Did you eat healthy today? ☐ yes ☐ no

Did you get enough sleep? ☐ yes ☐ no

Did you drink enough water? yes ☐ no

Did you take your vitamins/supplements? ☐ yes ☐ no

Spiritual

Did you do your Bible reading today? ☐ yes ☐ no

What did you read?

Did you pray today? ☐ yes ☐ no

What did you pray about?

No X-Cuses!

Mental/Emotional

What positive books/magazines did you read?

Did you spend personal thought-time today? ☐ yes ☐ no

What positive words did you speak to others?

What positive CDs did you listen to?

FEAR

"You can't walk by faith if you live in fear."
—a church marquee

I have been blessed to have worked as a counselor for troubled young men. During those years, I was taught much about life from them. One of them even felt compelled to teach me how to "hot-wire" a car (knowledge I have yet to put into practice). During one of our group sessions, I heard a young man make a statement I will never forget. Rodney said, "Fear isn't born; it is created." What profound wisdom from a young man!

Our fears are created. They are created based upon our past experiences. Based upon truth or not, our fears dictate our lives. They keep us from living up to our full potential.

One of my greatest fears is based upon my past. As a younger boy, I watched my sister being attacked by two dogs. It was severe enough that my sister required medical attention. Thus, the fear of being bitten has always played upon my mind.

My fear manifested itself one day as I was out for a morning run. I looked and saw a dog about a quarter of a mile ahead of me. The dog was standing boldly in the middle of the sidewalk. In that brief moment, I could only think about how fearful I was of dog attacks. I had never seen this dog before, and I did not know what kind of temperament he had. I was still thinking the worst based upon my fear. What opportunities have you and I missed out on because of fear?

I decided to run on anyway. The dog was wagging his tail as I passed him. How many of our fears never materialize? As I saw that dog from a distance, I was tempted to turn around and end my run early. Thankfully, I faced my fears head on. As it turned out, the fear was only alive in my thoughts. I ended up having an incredible run that morning. I would have cheated myself if I had I given into my fears.

I have developed a five stage process for me to overcome my fear:

1) Acknowledge the fear.

2) Feel the fear. Allow myself to have human emotions.

3) Recognize the worst possible outcome of my fears. Can my fear become a reality?

4) If so, what can I do to prevent it from happening?

5) Recognize that I am stronger than ANY fear I have!

ADDRESSING THE SPIRITUAL, PHYSICAL, AND MENTAL/EMOTIONAL:

What fears are you facing today? What fear is keeping you from following through on your goal? How are these fears affecting your spiritual life? Your mental/emotional life? Your physical life? Are these fears real? How have you magnified these fears? What steps can you take to overcome them and enjoy new success in your life?

Date_____

NO X-CUSES!

Journal

"If you knew who walked beside you at all times, you would
never experience fear again in your life."
—Dr. Wayne Dyer

_____
_____
_____
_____
_____
_____
_____
_____
_____
_____
_____
_____
_____
_____
_____
_____
_____
_____
_____
_____
_____
_____
_____
_____
_____
_____

Date_____

NO X-CUSES!

Physical

Did you exercise today? ☐ yes ☐ no

What exercise did you do?

Did you eat healthy today? ☐ yes ☐ no

Did you get enough sleep? ☐ yes ☐ no

Did you drink enough water? ☐ yes ☐ no

Did you take your vitamins/supplements? ☐ yes ☐ no

Spiritual

Did you do your Bible reading today? ☐ yes ☐ no

What did you read?

Did you pray today? ☐ yes ☐ no

What did you pray about?

Mental/Emotional

What positive books/magazines did you read?

Did you spend personal thought-time today? ☐ yes ☐ no

What positive words did you speak to others?

What positive CDs did you listen to?

QUIET TIME

In silence, we find the power to defeat any problem."
—Nick Perkins

Have you ever been awakened in the middle of the night? If you are content on engaging in sleep, then this can be a frustrating experience. I have found these times to be quite invigorating. The thing our souls may need more than anything else could be quiet meditation. Although sleep is good, quiet time is what connects our soul to our God.

I was awakened one morning (October 2, 2006) at four o'clock. I found myself wide awake; however, it was different this morning. I did not feel the urgency to do, just to be. Deep inside my soul, I wanted to be intimately quiet with myself. I walked outside to find a brisk October morning. In the solitude, I was connected to all the things around me.

The irony was strange. Although I was not doing anything, I felt more alive than ever. In the distance, I heard the cars passing by. The solitude was broken by the occasional falling of an acorn. When it is totally quiet, those little acorns can be very distracting. This placid tranquility even caused the stars to appear brighter. The silence allowed me to connect to that which was outside of me. I felt at one with the creation.

Quietness is something our souls cry for but very seldom receives. My yearly schedule provides me the opportunity for a quiet retreat. I leave the cell phone, the radio and television, the computer, and all the other distractions in order to spend time with myself. I must confess that I do bring my laptop—only for the purpose of writing.

At the request of my friend, Dr. Murphy Thomas, I have integrated quiet times into my yearly routine. At his urging, I have even spent time at a monastery. The monks taught me how precious solitude is. The first time I visited the monks, the silence intimidated me. I spent the grand total of three hours at the monastery, before I had to leave. The silence was too loud! In order to be the most effective, my soul has to have a steady diet of quietness. Does your soul need more quiet moments?

Taking this yearly silent retreat has taught me four important things:

1) To be thankful for everything I have (the good and the bad).

2) That I have been "fearfully and wonderfully" made.

3) Causes me to recognize the ways in which God takes care of me on a daily basis.

4) We, as a society, undervalue the rewards of silence.

ADDRESSING THE SPIRITUAL, PHYSICAL, AND MENTAL/EMOTIONAL:

In what ways can you benefit from more quiet time? How can quiet time benefit you in your mental/emotional, spiritual, and physical lives? What practical things can you do (on a daily basis) in order to find time to be quiet? Is there a specific place which allows you the opportunity to be still, reflect, and meditate?

Date_____

NO X-CUSES!

Journal

"All of man's troubles stem from his inability to sit quietly in a
room alone."
—Blaise Paschal

_____
_____
_____
_____
_____
_____
_____
_____
_____
_____
_____
_____
_____
_____
_____
_____
_____
_____
_____
_____
_____
_____
_____
_____
_____
_____
_____
_____
_____
_____
_____

Date_____

NO X-CUSES!

Physical

Did you exercise today? ☐ yes ☐ no

What exercise did you do?

Did you eat healthy today? ☐ yes ☐ no

Did you get enough sleep? ☐ yes ☐ no

Did you drink enough water? ☐ yes ☐ no

Did you take your vitamins/supplements? ☐ yes ☐ no

Spiritual

Did you do your Bible reading today? ☐ yes ☐ no

What did you read?

Did you pray today? ☐ yes ☐ no

What did you pray about?

Mental/Emotional

What positive books/magazines did you read?

Did you spend personal thought-time today? ☐ yes ☐ no

What positive words did you speak to others?

What positive CDs did you listen to?

Day 30

UNITY

"This above all: to thine own self be true; and it must follow,
as the night the day: Thou canst not then be false to any man."
—William Shakespeare

Unfortunately, we are a divided people. We are divided along many different fronts. Race, religion, and socio-economic status are just a few ways in which society tends to divide us. I challenge those divisions! I have come to realize that all human beings have more similarities than differences. Regretfully, we spend more time magnifying those differences.

My life experiences have allowed me to spend time with many people, who, on the surface, would appear to be much different than I am. I served many years as a pastor of rural, country churches. It was in these churches that I experienced a laid-back, take it easy lifestyle. On the other end of the spectrum, I spent some time working with inner-city youth, many from economically-depressed homes. It was from them I learned a new culture and vocabulary. Spending several years as an adolescent counselor, I communicated with kids who had a mentality that was very unique. From them, I learned compassion and acceptance.

Various cultures and countries have exposed me to different human tendencies. Sadly to say, many of us never realize how much alike we really are. It was Lulu who taught me most about togetherness. Lulu's funeral just happened to be my classroom experience.

Lulu was a broke (we can be broke financially, but not poor), African-American man who lived in a town where I pastored. He was quiet and stayed mostly to himself. His death was unexpected. Being from such a small community (300 people), we attended every funeral out of a sense of respect.

I attended Lulu's funeral. Out of respect for my position as a pastor, I was asked to speak a few words. It was an honor! I looked and saw what my African-American brother, Stephen Handy, calls "the rainbow." I saw white, black, poor, rich, and all between. What brought us together? It was not only to respect Lulu's life. It was to acknowledge that, in death, we are not different at all!

The simple things we can do to unify:

1) Figuratively, put on the other man or woman's shoes.

2) Recognize the breaks that we have experienced in our own life.

3) Take action to help someone else. Because of southern hospitality, we have a saying, "If there is anything I can do to help, then let me know." During the death of a friend's father, Ronnie Bonner never asked what he could do to help. He became proactive. He washed his friend's car. Why? He didn't want his friend to have a dirty car for the funeral processional. Bonner said it was the one thing he could do.

ADDRESSING THE SPIRITUAL, PHYSICAL, AND MENTAL/EMOTIONAL:

In what ways can you embrace the similarities you have with others? Are you spending any time with people who are "different" from you? What can you learn from them? What can you teach them? What does this say about your spiritual life?

Date_____

NO X-CUSES!

Journal

"We must learn to live together as brothers or perish together as fools."
—Dr. Martin Luther King, Jr.

_____

_____

_____

_____

_____

_____

_____

_____

_____

_____

_____

_____

_____

_____

_____

_____

_____

_____

_____

_____

_____

_____

_____

_____

_____

_____

_____

Date_____

NO X-CUSES!

Physical

Did you exercise today? ☐ yes ☐ no

What exercise did you do?

Did you eat healthy today? ☐ yes ☐ no

Did you get enough sleep? ☐ yes ☐ no

Did you drink enough water? ☐ yes ☐ no

Did you take your vitamins/supplements? ☐ yes ☐ no

Spiritual

Did you do your Bible reading today? ☐ yes ☐ no

What did you read?

Did you pray today? ☐ yes ☐ no

What did you pray about?

Mental/Emotional

What positive books/magazines did you read?

Did you spend personal thought-time today? ☐ yes ☐ no

What positive words did you speak to others?

What positive CDs did you listen to?

THE IMPORTANT QUESTIONS

"Know thyself."
—Socrates

Without a doubt, the most colorful individual to ever grace my life is Dr. Maurice Roberts. His 6'4" frame overflowed with laughter and joy. He could say one thing at the right time and have everyone laughing. His personality was endless.

Dr. Roberts would often quote his maxim for living. He would say, "The three most important questions in life: Where are you? Where have you been? And where are you going?" He always said if a person knew these three questions, then they would be a success. In retrospect, I did not understand him at the time. Now, with the help of time and wisdom (I hope I have acquired some), I think I understand his philosophy.

It is so healthy for each of us to take an accounting of our lives. My favorite quote of Socrates is, "An unexamined life is not worth living!" It is so important to know where we are in our lives. Are we at the place we want to be? Have we accomplished the goals we have set for ourselves? As important as this is to know, we often do not take the time to pursue the answers. These are important things for us to know.

Where have you been? Take inventory of your experiences. Chances are, you have already experienced more than you really even recognize. This question pervades all aspects of your life. From where have you come? Are there dramatic experiences you have had which have helped to define you as a person? Are there things that you have experienced in the past that could help someone else? Are you sharing those experiences? Our past often contains the keys of success for our future.

Where are you going? Proverbs 29:18 states, "Where there is no vision, the people perish." (kjv) Dr. Roberts impressed upon us the importance of having this mindset. You have to know where you are headed in order to get there. This question is extremely important for each of us. Where are you going? Do you know what direction you are headed? If not, how will you ever know if you get there? Set some plans in place. Give yourself a CLEAR vision of what it is you want to accomplish. This assessment should be done at least two times annually using the help of your accountability partners.

ADDRESSING THE SPIRITUAL, PHYSICAL, AND MENTAL/EMOTIONAL:

Where are you? Where have you been? Where are you going? Relate these questions to all areas of your life: Physical, Spiritual, and Mental/Emotional.

Date_____

NO X-CUSES!

Journal

"Do not confuse motion and progress. A rocking horse keeps
moving but does not make any progress."
—Alfred A. Montapert

_____
_____
_____
_____
_____
_____
_____
_____
_____
_____
_____
_____
_____
_____
_____
_____
_____
_____
_____
_____
_____
_____
_____
_____
_____
_____

Date_____

NO X-CUSES!

Physical

Did you exercise today? ☐ yes ☐ no

What exercise did you do?

Did you eat healthy today? ☐ yes ☐ no

Did you get enough sleep? ☐ yes ☐ no

Did you drink enough water? ☐ yes ☐ no

Did you take your vitamins/supplements? ☐ yes ☐ no

Spiritual

Did you do your Bible reading today? ☐ yes ☐ no

What did you read?

Did you pray today? ☐ yes ☐ no

What did you pray about?

No X-Cuses!

Mental/Emotional

What positive books/magazines did you read?

Did you spend personal thought-time today? ☐ yes ☐ no

What positive words did you speak to others?

What positive CDs did you listen to?

Day 32

THE RIGHT MINDSET

"The last of the human freedoms: to choose one's attitude in
any given set of circumstances, to choose one's own way."
—Viktor Frankl

Have you ever met a person who could brighten a dark room? Do you know what I am referring to? Some people are so positive and compassionate they make everything better around them. I am attempting to be one of those people.

Jean Harris was the most positive, loving person I have ever met. Regardless of what was happening to her, Jean was upbeat and positive. She was the kind of person who could look at a half-empty glass and thank God for the glass. No matter what the circumstances, Jean was always thankful to be alive.

Jean had her share of troubles. Her health had deteriorated over the period of several years. Crippling arthritis was slowly leaving her body crumpled and distorted. She lived with an intense amount of pain; however, her positive attitude never changed.

I was Jean's pastor for four years. During that time, Jean was hospitalized multiple times. Several times, I did not think she would survive. Every time, she bounced back. The time came when she began to deteriorate quickly.

She became critical and had to be taken to Johns Hopkins Hospital in Baltimore. Even though I could not go see her, I called her daily. I telephoned a fellow clergy who visited her frequently. Even though he had never met her before this, he commented on her positive attitude.

During this hospitalization, Jean had complications. The doctors decided she had to have her leg amputated. I often wondered why this had to happen to her, yet she never expressed those kinds of thoughts. The morning of her surgery, I called to pray with her. She started asking me about others in the church that needed her prayers. She said, "Brother Mark, there are people who are much sicker than I am." That statement epitomized her positive attitude.

The four things Jean Harris taught me about life:

1) We are never promised tomorrow. Make the most of today.

2) We set the tone for our own attitude (just look around, someone always has it worse).

3) A smile can change the universe. It is our responsibility to lighten the load for others and many times that can be done with a smile.

4) God will always take care of us.

ADDRESSING THE SPIRITUAL, PHYSICAL, AND MENTAL/EMOTIONAL:

Is it difficult for you to see the positive in life? How can you train your mind to see the positive? How can you rely on your spiritual life to change your mindset? How can this positive mindset affect your whole life? What can you do to become the positive person who brightens life for others?

Date_____

NO X-CUSES!

Journal

"Keep your face to the sunshine and you cannot see the
shadows."
—Helen Keller

_____
_____
_____
_____
_____
_____
_____
_____
_____
_____
_____
_____
_____
_____
_____
_____
_____
_____
_____
_____
_____
_____
_____
_____
_____
_____
_____
_____

Date_____

NO X-CUSES!

Physical

Did you exercise today? ☐ yes ☐ no

What exercise did you do?

Did you eat healthy today? ☐ yes ☐ no

Did you get enough sleep? ☐ yes ☐ no

Did you drink enough water? ☐ yes ☐ no

Did you take your vitamins/supplements? ☐ yes ☐ no

Spiritual

Did you do your Bible reading today? ☐ yes ☐ no

What did you read?

Did you pray today? ☐ yes ☐ no

What did you pray about?

Mental/Emotional

What positive books/magazines did you read?

Did you spend personal thought-time today? ☐ yes ☐ no

What positive words did you speak to others?

What positive CDs did you listen to?

POSSIBILITIES OR PROBLEMS

Mountains or molehills . . . . A matter of perspective."
—Charles T. Chappell

As I have mentioned earlier, much of my professional career has been dedicated as a pastor. Having spent twelve years in professional ministry, I understand the challenges that plague the clergy. Regardless of their religious faith, most clergy are hard-working people wanting to live out their life's calling.

During my tenure as a pastor, I had an experience that taught me a valuable lesson about having a positive mindset. I was pastoring four country churches (yes, I did say four) at the same time. These churches were in southwestern, middle Tennessee. I lived thirty-five minutes from the local Wal-Mart. The joke was that we lived so far out in the country we had to import sunshine. It was a great community with great people.

In the Spring of 1998, we had a major flood. During that flood, it damaged one of the churches. Being a small membership church, the budget often contained limited funds. At the time, we had one hundred twenty eight dollars in the church treasury. With no flood insurance, I thought the future looked grim. I was looking at the circumstances and not the possibilities.

I walked into the church that morning and my mouth flew open. The water had damaged the church extensively. I remember walking across the bowed-up floors, smelling the stench from the flood waters. I was devastated. Because of the flood's wrath, I thought I was watching the death of a church. Luckily, the church is about people and not buildings.

Although things looked bad, I remembered the verse, "We do not have because we do not ask God (James 4:2)." I began to do what I do best—talk. I called the denomination's disaster relief coordinator, Clay Hall. He said, "Don't worry! The church will be repaired!" Clay had more faith than I did. It was repaired and looked better than I had remembered it. Clay taught me that current circumstances do not define us. Our faith and attitude defines them.

People came from everywhere to help. Some cooked lunch, some provided tools, and some provided labor. Everyone working together brought the church back to life. It is a testimony of what can be accomplished. As I think about that church, I am reminded to look past the problems and see the possibilities!

ADDRESSING THE SPIRITUAL, PHYSICAL, AND MENTAL/EMOTIONAL:

What situations, in your life, have you down? Are you so busy looking at the problems you cannot see the possibilities? What will it take from you to overcome these problems? How will your spiritual life need to improve? How will you need to grow physically? What will it take mentally and emotionally?

Date_____

NO X-CUSES!

Journal

"Don't tell God how big your problems are—Tell your
problems how big your God is."
—Reverend T.D. Jakes

_____
_____
_____
_____
_____
_____
_____
_____
_____
_____
_____
_____
_____
_____
_____
_____
_____
_____
_____
_____
_____
_____
_____
_____
_____
_____
_____
_____
_____
_____

Date_____

NO X-CUSES!

Physical

Did you exercise today? ☐ yes ☐ no

What exercise did you do?

Did you eat healthy today? ☐ yes ☐ no

Did you get enough sleep? ☐ yes ☐ no

Did you drink enough water? ☐ yes ☐ no

Did you take your vitamins/supplements? ☐ yes ☐ no

Spiritual

Did you do your Bible reading today? ☐ yes ☐ no

What did you read?

Did you pray today? ☐ yes ☐ no

What did you pray about?

Mental/Emotional

What positive books/magazines did you read?

Did you spend personal thought-time today? □ yes □ no

What positive words did you speak to others?

What positive CDs did you listen to?

Day 34

COURAGE

"Hard times don't create heroes. It is during the hard times
when the 'hero' within us is revealed."
—Bob Riley

I believe in everyday heroes. Because of our daily environments, we come in contact with people who are worthy of our respect. Jerry Mathis is one whose life screams of courage. Unfortunately, Jerry died while I was writing this book.

Jerry spent three tours in Vietnam. Because he and a friend were in legal trouble as adolescents, Jerry was told he could not sign up for the Army. The draft called his number, and the rest is history. Jerry retired after serving twenty one years, one month, and twenty nine days in the Army.

When I think about courage, I think about Jerry. In 1966, he was a naïve, nineteen-year old that went from the security of a country farm to the treachery of the Vietnam jungle. While many different emotions were flowing through him, Jerry admits to being both excited and scared. Although fearful, Jerry never once thought of avoiding his duty to serve the country.

Because of our friendship, I talked to Jerry extensively about his Army career. Most veterans who have seen combat very seldom talk about those experiences. From time to time, Jerry has shared some of those experiences. Because of those conversations, I know how courageous Jerry really was. On one occasion, Jerry told me about the time he had to shoot and kill someone, because they were attempting to kill his platoon members. After killing the enemy, his platoon congratulated him. Afterwards, he went to the edge of the camp and regurgitated. He said, "I was sick to my stomach, but I had to do it." I cannot imagine the horror of having to kill another human being. That night, Jerry's courage saved the lives of several others.

Despite his courage, Jerry was unwelcome when he returned home. He was cursed and spit upon. I only wished people then could have heard Tom Brokaw's words, "You can hate the war, but not the warrior." Jerry is one of those warriors.

In spite of his fear, Jerry still fulfilled his duties. He faced challenges most of us will never be able to comprehend. In spite of that, he stood boldly. If he could do that, what is our excuse?

ADDRESSING THE SPIRITUAL, PHYSICAL, AND MENTAL/EMOTIONAL:

Define courage. What fears would you have to face in order to demonstrate courage? In your own eyes, how could you be more courageous? What spiritual mindset would you need in order for this to happen?

Date_____

NO X-CUSES!

Journal

"Courage is doing what you're afraid to do. There can be no
courage unless you're scared."
—Eddie Rickenbacker

Date_____

NO X-CUSES!

Physical

Did you exercise today? ☐ yes ☐ no

What exercise did you do?

Did you eat healthy today? ☐ yes ☐ no

Did you get enough sleep? ☐ yes ☐ no

Did you drink enough water? ☐ yes ☐ no

Did you take your vitamins/supplements? ☐ yes ☐ no

Spiritual

Did you do your Bible reading today? ☐ yes ☐ no

What did you read?

Did you pray today? ☐ yes ☐ no

What did you pray about?

Mental/Emotional

What positive books/magazines did you read?

Did you spend personal thought-time today? ☐ yes ☐ no

What positive words did you speak to others?

What positive CDs did you listen to?

TENACITY

"To make our way, we must have firm resolve, persistence,
tenacity. We must gear ourselves to work hard all the way. We
can never let up."
—Ralph Bunche

We have an old expression in the South. It says, "It is not the
size of the dog in the fight, it is the size of the fight in the dog that
counts." I am reminded of my friend, Don Austin, when I hear or
see that quote. Together, Don and I served a church. He was the
Christian Education minister, and I was the associate minister and
youth minister.

Although we shared the same birthday (May 27th), we were
total opposites. Being thirty-five years older than I, his experience
and wisdom were more developed than mine. Don was absolutely,
without a shadow of a doubt, the most stubborn man I have ever
known. His stubbornness led him to be tenacious about the things
in which he believed strongly. They are characteristics I admired
greatly.

Although his stubbornness and tenacity often landed him in
trouble with church members, these characteristics extended his life.
Due to a brain tumor, Don's last days were horrific. Although he had
had a rough battle, I never witnessed anyone who fought as hard as
he did. Don may have had cancer, but Don never allowed cancer to
have him. Even though cancer may have won the fight, Don died,
just like he lived, with great tenacity.

The lessons Don Austin taught me are too numerous to list. He
taught me four that I will never forget:

1) Develop thick skin. It does not matter what others say about
   you.

2) Our ultimate responsibility is to God.

3) Forgive easily. Let things go and then move on. As my grandmother said, "Let things slide, like pouring water off a duck's back."

4) Our lives play a bigger part in the universe than we think they do. Take life seriously.

ADDRESSING THE SPIRITUAL, PHYSICAL, AND MENTAL/EMOTIONAL:

What battles are you fighting today? How can you maintain the tenacity to make it? What convictions can give you the tenacity to make it even when it looks hopeless?

Date_____

NO X-CUSES!

Journal

"Let me tell you the secret that has led me to my goal. My
strength lies solely in my tenacity."
—Louis Pasteur

Date_____

NO X-CUSES!

Physical

Did you exercise today? ☐ yes ☐ no

What exercise did you do?

Did you eat healthy today? ☐ yes ☐ no

Did you get enough sleep? ☐ yes ☐ no

Did you drink enough water? ☐ yes ☐ no

Did you take your vitamins/supplements? ☐ yes ☐ no

Spiritual

Did you do your Bible reading today? ☐ yes ☐ no

What did you read?

Did you pray today? ☐ yes ☐ no

What did you pray about?

Mental/Emotional

What positive books/magazines did you read?

Did you spend personal thought-time today? ☐ yes ☐ no

What positive words did you speak to others?

What positive CDs did you listen to?

Day 36

THE RIGHT FUEL

"Don't dig your grave with your own knife and fork."
—English Proverb

Due to youthful mistakes, we learn how to be the most productive. I learned such a lesson from my faithful Dodge truck. Without paying attention, I once filled my truck up with the wrong type of fuel. Being a gasoline-powered engine, my truck did not agree with my mistake.

I was traveling through a small Alabama town, when I needed to stop in order to refuel. Without noticing, I grabbed the pump handle and filled up my fuel tank. Because of my lack of focus, I failed to notice the diesel labeling on the gas pump. The real value for mistakes is that we learn from them. Because of that day, I always make sure what kind of fuel goes into my vehicle.

As I pulled away from the gas station that day, everything seemed normal. Just two miles down the road, my truck began to knock and ping. It had never acted in such a way. After all, I drove a Dodge truck. Dodge trucks are built RAM tough . . . provided they are fed properly!

Luckily, I found an honest mechanic. He quickly diagnosed my dilemma. Even though it was a bad mistake on my part, he did not treat me as a dumb college kid. My truck received a drained tank and a friendly refueling (with the right fuel) for a modest price. A great solution was found for a lousy predicament.

Even though our vehicles are expensive, sometimes, we do not give them the proper fuel. Likewise, our bodies need proper nutrition in order to function well. After all, it takes a vast amount of nutrition to fuel our bodies throughout our daily schedules. If we do not feed our bodies correctly, then we are asking for trouble.

Nutritional experts continue to confirm the benefits of healthy eating. From my own life, I realize the difference between eating healthily and choosing to eat quick and easy. My body talks to me. If I eat fast food laced with fats and carbohydrates, then I feel sluggish and suffer with diminished energy.

Our bodies are complicated machines and must be maintained meticulously. In order to function at high energy levels, we must eat naturally. After all, there are no substitutes for good fruits and vegetables. As in the example of my truck, if I put in the right fuel, then my body responds in a positive manner. If I choose to eat junk, then I choose to live life without the prime energy level I could have, thus making things harder than they should be.

ADDRESSING THE SPIRITUAL, PHYSICAL, AND MENTAL/EMOTIONAL:

Do you eat healthily? How could you improve your diet? In what ways does your diet affect the rest of your life? How can I improve the three areas of my life by improving my eating habits?

Date_____

NO X-CUSES!

Journal

"We think fast food is equivalent to pornography, nutritionally
speaking."
—Steve Elbert

Date_____

NO X-CUSES!

Physical

Did you exercise today? ☐ yes ☐ no

What exercise did you do?

Did you eat healthy today? ☐ yes ☐ no

Did you get enough sleep? ☐ yes ☐ no

Did you drink enough water? ☐ yes ☐ no

Did you take your vitamins/supplements? ☐ yes ☐ no

Spiritual

Did you do your Bible reading today? ☐ yes ☐ no

What did you read?

Did you pray today? ☐ yes ☐ no

What did you pray about?

Mental/Emotional

What positive books/magazines did you read?

Did you spend personal thought-time today? ☐ yes ☐ no

What positive words did you speak to others?

What positive CDs did you listen to?

CREATING LEADERS

"Effective leadership is not about making speeches or being
liked; leadership is defined by results not attributes."
—Peter Drucker

By interacting with others, I have been taught a wealth of knowledge. Everyday experiences give us the opportunity to learn from others. If adults will allow them, young people can be great teachers. By allowing adolescents to lead, we give them the opportunity to change their lives.

I have spent much of my life working with young people. Young people are open to adults who will really listen to what they say. Most young people, like most adults, will live up to the level of expectation placed upon them. To our mistake, many adults expect very little out of young people.

During part of my life, I found great joy in being a substitute teacher for a local school district. Many substitute teachers have a difficult time controlling the class. However, I have never had that problem. Young people have always been very respectful and courteous to me. To my credit, I expect only the best behavior from them. To this point, they have always responded in a positive manner.

During one day of substitute teaching duty, I was supposed to have a spirited class. The teacher left me a note containing three young men's names. On that note, she stated these young men would cause me a great deal of confusion. As I read that note, I doubted I would have the same experience. Those young men's behavior matched my expectation level.

As the young people entered the classroom, I addressed each young man in a one-on-one conversation. I told each one, "I understand you are a leader in this class. The rest of the class will do what you do. You set the tone in this classroom. Today, I need your help. I need you to do what you are supposed to do. I need you to be a leader in a positive way. Can you help me?" Each young man responded that they would. I also told them, "I believe you are a man of your word." They lived up to their leadership abilities.

Those young men are leaders. Every day, they prove their leadership ability. They lead in either a positive or negative way. I provided for them an opportunity to lead in a positive way. They responded magnificently.

There are leaders all around us. Even if they are influencing others in a negative way, they are still leaders. It is our responsibility to create as many positive leaders as possible. We are given opportunities to help others discover their positive leadership ability. Let us take seriously the responsibility with which we have been entrusted.

In order to produce leaders, I have found:

1) Communication is vital. I must state my expectations clearly.

2) I must empower my leaders to lead. It is of paramount importance to give them the tools they need to lead in the most efficient way. To do otherwise, would be setting them up for failure.

3) Regardless of age, always show respect. This means that I have to trust my future leaders to make mistakes and to learn from them.

ADDRESSING THE SPIRITUAL, PHYSICAL, AND MENTAL/EMOTIONAL:

Are you creating leaders? How are you providing others the opportunity to discover their leadership ability? Why is it your spiritual responsibility to do so? How have you changed the world by creating leadership in others?

Date_____

NO X-CUSES!

Journal

"Leaders don't create followers, they create more leaders."
—Tom Peters

_____
_____
_____
_____
_____
_____
_____
_____
_____
_____
_____
_____
_____
_____
_____
_____
_____
_____
_____
_____
_____
_____
_____
_____
_____
_____
_____

Date_____

NO X-CUSES!

Physical

Did you exercise today? ☐ yes ☐ no

What exercise did you do?

Did you eat healthy today? ☐ yes ☐ no

Did you get enough sleep? ☐ yes ☐ no

Did you drink enough water? ☐ yes ☐ no

Did you take your vitamins/supplements? ☐ yes ☐ no

Spiritual

Did you do your Bible reading today? ☐ yes ☐ no

What did you read?

Did you pray today? ☐ yes ☐ no

What did you pray about?

Mental/Emotional

What positive books/magazines did you read?

Did you spend personal thought-time today? ☐ yes ☐ no

What positive words did you speak to others?

What positive CDs did you listen to?

WHY NOT ME?

"High achievement always takes place in the framework of
high expectation."
—Charles F. Kettering

One of my favorite movies is *Dreamer*. The story is based upon a true story about a horse that makes a comeback after breaking a leg. The plot of the movie revolves around a little girl and the love for her horse. Tugging at my heart's strings, I always find the movie inspirational.

After the horse recovers from a broken leg, it is apparent she has the chance to be very successful. The little girl, played by Dakota Fanning, becomes excited about the possibilities. During a family meeting, she shares her dreams for the future. She states that somebody has to race in the Breeder's Cup. Her next line echoes in my mind. She simply said, "Why not us?" Her family and friends supported her dreams. They uplifted and encouraged her to go after success.

As I think about that line, I bring it to the personal level. Thinking about my dreams, I say, "Why not me?" Somebody has to do it. Besides myself, I can think of no one else I would like to accomplish my dreams and goals.

Who would you like to see accomplish your goals and dreams? Is there something limiting you from accomplishing them? If you wish to accomplish your goals, then you need to begin by asking, "Why not me?" Expect the best!

To expect the best:

1) Renew your mind daily. The power of the Word is vitally clear in Romans 12:2. It simply states that if one wants to be

transformed then one must renew the mind. How do you do that? Add the positive; Subtract the negative. Nature abhors a vacuum. If you take something out, then you must replace it. Always, always, always replace the negative with the positive.

2) Positive support group. We are only as strong as the people around us. "The more wise counsel you follow, the better your chances." (Proverbs 11:14, The Message)

3) Speak it into existence. "Words kill, words give life; they're either poison or fruit—you choose." (Proverbs 18:24, The Message)

ADDRESSING THE SPIRITUAL, PHYSICAL, AND MENTAL/EMOTIONAL:

Do you feel deserving to accomplish your dreams? How would your life change if you asked, "Why not me?" How would it change your life spiritually, physically, and mentally/emotionally?

Date_____

NO X-CUSES!

Journal

"Our problem is not that we expect too much, but too little.
We are like ignorant children who want to go on making mud
pies in the slum because we cannot imagine what is meant by
the offer of a holiday at the sea. We are far too easily pleased."
—C.S. Lewis

Date_____

NO X-CUSES!

Physical

Did you exercise today? ☐ yes ☐ no

What exercise did you do?

Did you eat healthy today? ☐ yes ☐ no

Did you get enough sleep? ☐ yes ☐ no

Did you drink enough water? ☐ yes ☐ no

Did you take your vitamins/supplements? ☐ yes ☐ no

Spiritual

Did you do your Bible reading today? ☐ yes ☐ no

What did you read?

Did you pray today? ☐ yes ☐ no

What did you pray about?

Mental/Emotional

What positive books/magazines did you read?

Did you spend personal thought-time today? ☐ yes ☐ no

What positive words did you speak to others?

What positive CDs did you listen to?

FRIENDSHIP

"Be courteous to all, but intimate with few, and let those few
be well tried before you give them your confidence."
—George Washington

Alex Haley, the famed author of the Book *Roots* had a beautiful picture that hung in his office. The picture consisted of a turtle sitting on a fence post. Below the painting was a caption that read, "When you see a turtle on a fence post, you know he did not get there by himself." A true statement made about the picture and life.

We will never be able to achieve success in life without the help of others. It is impossible! The underlying fact of the universe is that we are all connected. We cannot be successful without helping someone else out along the way. The game of life just works that way. Nature teaches us this lesson with the example of the great sequoias. The tallest of all trees; however, their strength lies in the root system. They are interconnected. They draw strength from each other. When one of the trees becomes weak, the roots from the others keep it standing tall.

I have been blessed to always have supportive people in my life. All of the success I experience today is because of other people who have believed in me. My friend, Derek Peterson, calls this our "web" of support. We all need these people upon whom we can depend. Our support (our web) is our connection to our power and strength.

You have already received the help of someone else. Who has helped place you on top of the proverbial fence post? Who has given you help and support when you needed it most? Those are the people for whom we must be thankful. The mark of a powerful life is gratitude. Have you expressed that gratitude to someone in your life?

ADDRESSING THE SPIRITUAL, PHYSICAL, AND MENTAL/EMOTIONAL:

Giving thanks empowers us spiritually. Who do you have to be thankful for? How did they improve your life? Sit down <u>NOW</u> and send them a handwritten card to tell them "thank you" for what they did to improve your life.

Note: I encourage you to make this a regular practice. Try sending at least one note of thanks per week. People never expect it. It is a lost art form in our e-mail and text driven society.

Date_____

NO X-CUSES!

Journal

"When the character of a man is not clear to you, look at his
friends."
—Japanese Proverb

_____
_____
_____
_____
_____
_____
_____
_____
_____
_____
_____
_____
_____
_____
_____
_____
_____
_____
_____
_____
_____
_____
_____
_____
_____
_____
_____
_____
_____

Date_____

NO X-CUSES!

Physical

Did you exercise today? ☐ yes ☐ no

What exercise did you do?

Did you eat healthy today? ☐ yes ☐ no

Did you get enough sleep? ☐ yes ☐ no

Did you drink enough water? ☐ yes ☐ no

Did you take your vitamins/supplements? ☐ yes ☐ no

Spiritual

Did you do your Bible reading today? ☐ yes ☐ no

What did you read?

Did you pray today? ☐ yes ☐ no

What did you pray about?

Mental/Emotional

What positive books/magazines did you read?

Did you spend personal thought-time today? ☐ yes ☐ no

What positive words did you speak to others?

What positive CDs did you listen to?

Day 40

FORGIVENESS

"Always forgive your enemies: Nothing annoys them so
much."
—Oscar Wilde

Forgiveness is a powerful tool in our lives. Forgiveness empowers us while lack of forgiveness steals our energy and focus. There are two forms of forgiveness. The first form is perhaps the most difficult—forgiving ourselves. After we forgive ourselves, we must learn to forgive others. A lack of forgiveness causes us to focus on the past instead of the future.

Real, lasting forgiveness is a paradox in nature. At our core, we really do not want to forgive others for the mean and nasty things they have done to us. The only way to really forgive is to put it into practice. It is only when we do loving things for the person that we truly begin to feel forgiveness. We do loving things and then forgiveness happens. Unfortunately, we think it is the other way around.

Recently, I put this theory into practice. Against one person, I had held a grudge for over five years. I said I had forgiven him; however, by my attitude, I knew I had not done so. It was only after I began to reach out to that person that I began to feel forgiveness. As I showed acts of loving kindness towards him, my attitude began to change. I actually like him again. The action came first and then the attitude change followed. Sounds crazy but that is the way it sometimes works. The Lord's Prayer states that we want God to forgive us in the same way we forgive others. When it is put that way, we find the necessity to forgive all others.

Forgiveness says so much about our lives:

1) When we forgive, we are saying that we are forward thinking. Forgiveness always demands that the future will be better than the past.

2) It says that we are outward thinking towards other people. We are willing to put other people first. We never really know all the reasons a person does or says something. If we were in the same situation, who knows what we would do!

3) It says I am reminded of my own imperfections. It provides me the opportunity to embrace my own humanness, not for an excuse, but for a definition. When we understand our humanness, we allow other people to make mistakes. It is called grace—how the world needs more of it!

ADDRESSING THE SPIRITUAL, PHYSICAL, AND MENTAL/EMOTIONAL:

Who do you need to forgive? Why? In what ways can you do loving acts for them? How has your life been hurt by your lack of willingness to forgive others?

Date_____

NO X-CUSES!

Journal

"Forgiveness is not mine to give. In order to receive the greatness of God, I must let go of other people's misdemeanors."
—Mark Beecham

_____

_____

_____

_____

_____

_____

_____

_____

_____

_____

_____

_____

_____

_____

_____

_____

_____

_____

_____

_____

_____

_____

Date_____

NO X-CUSES!

Physical

Did you exercise today? ☐ yes ☐ no

What exercise did you do?

Did you eat healthy today? ☐ yes ☐ no

Did you get enough sleep? ☐ yes ☐ no

Did you drink enough water? ☐ yes ☐ no

Did you take your vitamins/supplements? ☐ yes ☐ no

Spiritual

Did you do your Bible reading today? ☐ yes ☐ no

What did you read?

Did you pray today? ☐ yes ☐ no

What did you pray about?

Mental/Emotional

What positive books/magazines did you read?

Did you spend personal thought-time today? ☐ yes ☐ no

What positive words did you speak to others?

What positive CDs did you listen to?

TRUTH AND FREEDOM

"In the truest sense, freedom cannot be bestowed; it must be
achieved."
—Franklin D. Roosevelt

Abraham Lincoln once illustrated to a young man how important truth was. He asked the young man, "How many legs does a cow have?" To which the young man replied, "Four." President Lincoln then asked, "Suppose you call the cow's tail a leg, then how many legs would the cow have?" The young man confidentially responded, "Five." President Lincoln, showing his wisdom, said, "Young man, that is where you are wrong. Calling a cow's tail a leg does not make it a leg." The truth made plain and simple.

Several years ago, I was involved in a twelve-step recovery group. It was a truly remarkable experience. Almost every week, I witnessed people make profound discoveries about themselves. What makes that possible? I believe it is because of one underlying covenant made between each individual in the group: Complete honesty. No fertilizer allowed! (Ask a farmer for the explanation).

Over that year, I witnessed a first-hand view of freedom. Sadly to say, our society tends to view freedom in terms of material wealth. While that may be a component of freedom, it is not the most important. Freedom is the ability to completely be who God created you to be. Freedom comes only after being truthful about yourself and then allowing God to do the changing!

Freedom is a long, hard road. Over the past year, I have witnessed the life of a friend. During that time, I saw her grow into a completely different person. Her change is quite obvious: She is free from her addictions of alcohol and drugs. Her freedom allows herself to enjoy the great things in life.

What has caused her to enjoy this freedom? Knowing her so well, I could testify that her faith is at the very core of her freedom. After truthfully and whole-heartedly working the twelve-steps, she discovered she was not in control of her life. She knew she had to give control over to the care of God.

Working the twelve-steps, one must be completely truthful about who they are. Step four says, "We made a searching and fearless moral inventory of ourselves." Is that easy to do? No. All of us are guilty of playing games with ourselves. We do not want to "call a spade a spade." During this process, the truth allows all of us to see who we really are and who God wants us to be. Oscar Wilde said it best, "It is the confession, not the priest, that gives us absolution." Being truthful, we allow ourselves to experience real freedom.

One thing that I have learned about truth and freedom:

1) Truth always triumphs over fear. "Fear is not born; it is created." I heard an adolescent say that one day, and it could very well be the wisest thing I have ever heard from a teenager. Fear is often just a mirage to keep us from the truth. One must overcome fear in order to enjoy truth and freedom.

ADDRESSING THE SPIRITUAL, PHYSICAL, AND MENTAL/EMOTIONAL:

What do you need to be truthful about? If you were really truthful about your life, what would change? Being honest and truthful would rid yourself of false guilt and provide forgiveness. Being completely honest, how would your life experience freedom?

Date_____

NO X-CUSES!

Journal

"It is for freedom that Christ has set us free. Stand firm, then, and do not let yourselves be burdened again by a yoke of slavery."
—Galatians 5:1

_____
_____
_____
_____
_____
_____
_____
_____
_____
_____
_____
_____
_____
_____
_____
_____
_____
_____
_____
_____
_____
_____
_____
_____
_____
_____
_____

Date_____

NO X-CUSES!

Physical

Did you exercise today? ☐ yes ☐ no

What exercise did you do?

Did you eat healthy today? ☐ yes ☐ no

Did you get enough sleep? ☐ yes ☐ no

Did you drink enough water? ☐ yes ☐ no

Did you take your vitamins/supplements? ☐ yes ☐ no

Spiritual

Did you do your Bible reading today? ☐ yes ☐ no

What did you read?

Did you pray today? ☐ yes ☐ no

What did you pray about?

Mental/Emotional

What positive books/magazines did you read?

Did you spend personal thought-time today? ☐ yes ☐ no

What positive words did you speak to others?

What positive CDs did you listen to?

Day 42

RULES FOR LIFE

"Rules are for the obedience of fools and the guidance of wise men."
—Douglas Bader

Our children are our greatest teachers. If only we will listen, they are waiting to teach. The real power is they do not even know they are so wise. Look around and learn from them how to really live. The mark of a wise man is that he learns from others regardless of their age.

I learned a valuable lesson from a group of five and six-year olds. My five-year old friend was the ring leader of this group. He was playing organized baseball for the first time in his life. Being much like he, the rest of the team did not know all the rules of the game. They knew how to hit, run, and catch. It was fun just watching them have so much fun.

Being unsure of what the exact rules were, they sometimes ran and were tagged out when they could have stayed on the base. It was a mistake that seemed to occur quite often. They really did not seem to care. All they wanted to do was hit the ball, run, and have fun. Their joyful attitude overshadowed any mistakes they made.

As I watched them play, I realized the experience was really a metaphor for life. We don't have to know all the rules. We just have to listen to our coach and love the game. The rest we will learn in time—that is called wisdom. After watching them, I realized we all have basic rules we have to follow.

My rules dictate how I choose to play the game of life. My rules are as follows:

1. Love God first and most.

2. Be Honest.—George Washington said, "I cannot tell a lie." Actually, he could have, but he CHOSE not to do so.

3. Treat others the way I want to be treated.

4. Be Positive. No matter how dark a situation looks, I can learn something.

5. I am strongest when I tell others, "I LOVE YOU!" and "I AM SORRY. I MESSED UP."

ADDRESSING THE SPIRITUAL, PHYSICAL, AND MENTAL/EMOTIONAL:

What are your five basic rules that pattern your life physically, mental/emotionally, and spiritually? Can people look at your life and see these rules being put into practice?

Date_____

NO X-CUSES!

Journal

"When I approach a child, he inspires in me two sentiments: tenderness for what he is, and respect for what he may become."
—Louis Pasteur

_____
_____
_____
_____
_____
_____
_____
_____
_____
_____
_____
_____
_____
_____
_____
_____
_____
_____
_____
_____
_____
_____
_____
_____
_____
_____

Date_____

NO X-CUSES!

Physical

Did you exercise today? ☐ yes ☐ no

What exercise did you do?

Did you eat healthy today? ☐ yes ☐ no

Did you get enough sleep? ☐ yes ☐ no

Did you drink enough water? ☐ yes ☐ no

Did you take your vitamins/supplements? ☐ yes ☐ no

Spiritual

Did you do your Bible reading today? ☐ yes ☐ no

What did you read?

Did you pray today? ☐ yes ☐ no

What did you pray about?

Mental/Emotional

What positive books/magazines did you read?

Did you spend personal thought-time today? ☐ yes ☐ no

What positive words did you speak to others?

What positive CDs did you listen to?

FOLLOW-UP

"The beginning is the most important part of the work."
—Plato

After completing the past forty-two days, how has your life changed? Have you accomplished the goals you set out to accomplish? How have you concentrated your life more fully on the spiritual, physical, and mental/emotional aspects? Have you developed a daily "game plan" which will help you address the three aspects of your life? What are they?

FINAL THOUGHTS

Eric Johnson said, "Every man in reality is two men: the man he is, and the man he could be." Change is possible! After engaging in the No X-Cuses! Lifestyle for the past forty-two days, it is my prayer that you have started on a new path to being a new person. Life is about developing new habits which lead us to new actions.

Every day, I encourage you to do something to enrich your life spiritually, physically, and mentally/emotionally. Your discipline to do so will pay dividends. In my observations, people who address these issues on a daily basis are the ones that achieve real success in life. Only you can do it.

I leave you with the words of Isaiah the prophet: "But those who hope in the Lord will renew their strength. They will soar on wings like eagles; they will run and not grow weary, they will walk and not faint (Isaiah 40:31)." The strength is there. Will you take it? Will you decide to live a life with absolutely No X-Cuses?

-Mark Beecham
April 19, 2012

IN MEMORY

During the writing of this book, some very important people died: Tim Griffith, Reverend Johnny Adams, Reverend Jerry Mathis, Reverend Don Austin and my brother, Michael Beecham. May they always be remembered for the lives they changed.

Please check out our website for other publications, audio resources, and daily blogs:

www.noxcuse.org

Mark Beecham is a proud alumnus of Martin Methodist College where he received his B.A. degree in Biblical Studies. Being a Zimmerman Scholar in Residence recipient, Mark also studied at Hebrew University in Jerusalem, Israel. He is also an alumnus of Asbury Theological Seminary in Wilmore, Kentucky. After serving as a pastor/youth pastor, Mark developed No X-Cuse! Seminars LLC, a motivational and life coaching business. Using his goal setting and follow-through principles, he has completed two marathons and is currently preparing for his first triathlon. He is currently writing his third book, *Wisdom from the Rearview Mirror*. He has been able to share these principles by speaking nationally and internationally. Wanting to be the best he can be, Mark has been mentored by the best in the business: Les Brown, Ona Brown, and Dr. Harold Sweeting, just to name a few. Some of Mark's clients include leaders from major U.S. corporations. In his spare time, Mark enjoys skiing, playing guitar, and writing. In 2004, he wrote and published *A Cracked Pot*, a book about his own struggles to overcome the effects of childhood sexual abuse. He is an avid runner and cyclist and a big University of Tennessee football fan; however, his greatest claim to fame is being a proud uncle to his nephews, Spencer and Chandler.

CPSIA information can be obtained at www.ICGtesting.com
Printed in the USA
LVOW040157131012

302671LV00001B/8/P